The Highly Effective Office

The Highly Effective Office

Creating a Successful Lean Culture in Any Workplace

Timothy Schipper

Routledge
Taylor & Francis Group

A PRODUCTIVITY PRESS BOOK

First edition published in 2019
by Routledge/Productivity Press

52 Vanderbilt Avenue New York, NY 10017, USA
2 Park Square, Milton Park, Abingdon, Oxon OX14 4RN, UK

© 2019 by Taylor & Francis Group, LLC

Routledge/Productivity Press is an imprint of Taylor & Francis Group, an Informa business

No claim to original U.S. Government works
Printed on acid-free paper

International Standard Book Number-13: 978-1-138-34453-2 (Hardback)
International Standard Book Number-13: 978-0-429-43847-9 (eBook)

Library of Congress Cataloging-in-Publication Data

Names: Schipper, Timothy, author.
Title: The highly effective office : creating a successful lean culture in any workplace / Timothy Schipper.
Description: New York, NY : Routledge, [2019]
Identifiers: LCCN 2018044582 (print) | LCCN 2018046566 (ebook) | ISBN 9780429438479 (e-Book) | ISBN 9781138344532 (hardback : alk. paper)
Subjects: LCSH: Office management. | Organizational effectiveness. | Corporate culture. | Industrial management.
Classification: LCC HF5547 (ebook) | LCC HF5547 .S346 2019 (print) | DDC 651.3068/4–dc23
LC record available at https://lccn.loc.gov/2018044582

Visit the Taylor & Francis Web site at
http://www.taylorandfrancis.com

Contents

List of Figures

List of Tables

Foreword

I've worked with Tim Schipper for 15 years, most intensively during the 5 years of the Office Lean Consulting Team at Steelcase. Tim was one of the original members of the team and served throughout its existence. I was the team leader.

Tim has broad and deep knowledge of Lean, as a teacher, coach, practitioner in manufacturing, administrative, and technical-professional environments, and in new product and process developments. The Office Lean Consulting Team supported more than 150 cross-functional business process value stream improvement projects, each of which had to meet the criterion of spanning at least two departments. As Tim describes in the pages that follow, Lean in the office is all about cross-functional value streams.

We got our start on office Lean at Steelcase after over 10 years of Lean implementations in the company's manufacturing plants worldwide. But as Tim explains, Lean in office business processes is quite different from Lean in manufacturing. In a manufacturing plant, it is possible to assemble dedicated teams to make major changes quickly, in part because in a factory, one person is responsible for the whole building, greatly reducing the reluctance of department managers to free up a person for a time-limited project. That singular responsibility is very different from office, or business process, value streams, which are missing from org charts, cross internal "political" boundaries, have no dedicated resources, no budget, no measures, no clearly identified customer, and no one singularly responsible for leading, managing, and improving the process.

Our team had help at the outset, with staff from John Shook's TWI consulting network based at Michigan's Engineering College and from Drew Locher. Drew and TWI had had previous experience applying Lean thinking to enterprise business processes. From that starting point, the team engaged in continual PDCA, refining, documenting, and making improvements to our office Lean consulting practice. Tim was a major contributor and critical resource both in supporting the project teams we coached and in refining and improving our tools, training program, approaches, and measures.

In my work with Tim after I retired from Steelcase, I've see the fruits of his continuing focus on improving and streamlining the office Lean workshop process and tools. I have also been pleased to see the outcomes of Tim's continuing office Lean work at Steelcase, where, thanks to his influence, office Lean approaches have become "the way we do things around here."

What you'll read in this book is a wonderful reflection of the clarity of Tim's approach as a Lean teacher, coach, and workshop facilitator. His work is thoughtful, well organized, and accessible. He is effective and highly regarded as a Lean teacher. He has made significant contributions to the tools, practices, and overall approach of the Lean office workshop process and, importantly, to the process of refining and implementing the improvement plans from value stream workshops.

I wanted Tim to write this book. I'm glad he has. I'm confident you will be too.

David Mann, PhD
Grand Rapids, Michigan

Preface

In the summer of 2016, I was traveling with David Mann, my teacher and Lean sensei, to a well-known mid-west manufacturer. We were talking about the Lean office transformation that had occurred over the past dozen years at Steelcase. David (now retired from Steelcase) was telling me how rare it was to transfer Lean concepts from manufacturing to the office. Yet, we had done just that at Steelcase. Steelcase was founded in 1912 as the Metal Office Furniture Company in Grand Rapids, Michigan, and it is more than 105 years old. Its innovation legacy began in 1914 when it received its first patent for the manufacturing process developed to make a strong, durable, low-cost fireproof waste basket, a major innovation at that time. Looking back, it is clear that Steelcase has always been looking forward. The past, present, and future are all about turning insights into innovations that unlock the promise of people at work and make the world a better place. That innovative spirit continues to display itself in the transformation of business value streams using Lean principles and practices.

The office Lean program at Steelcase was launched in 2004 with David's steady hand at the helm leading the Lean office initiative. The effort then continued after his retirement in 2010 with the team that he handpicked and put in place.

David encouraged me by saying, "You know, you really should write a book about the Lean transformation in the office. There is a story to tell." On the office side at Steelcase, we went from the first crude, hand-drawn value stream maps in 2003 to an Office Lean Consulting Team that was established in 2004. The Steelcase team led the Lean transformation for the next 10 years within the company and achieved some significant results.

David encouraged me to write this book. I wasn't planning on writing another book anytime soon, but he recognized that there was a story to tell about the application of Lean principles beyond manufacturing and into the office. David's book, *Creating a Lean Culture* (CRC Press, 2015), described how the manufacturing system at Steelcase had been transformed by Lean. I had written about how to apply Lean to development in *Innovative Lean Development* (Productivity Press, 2010) with my colleague Mark Swets in 2009 while working with David at Steelcase. Although that was an enjoyable experience, I remembered the amount of time and effort it required. So, I wasn't actively planning a book project, but I had always entertained the notion in the back of my mind that I might write another book *someday*. David told me that if I didn't tell the story of the Lean office transformation and the techniques used to get there, the story might not ever be passed on to other organizations that would benefit as much as we at Steelcase and at some of the other organizations featured in the case studies of this book had.

The techniques to overcome the challenges of creating and sustaining a Lean culture in manufacturing are thoroughly and expertly described in David's book *Creating a Lean Culture: Tools to Sustain Lean*. His book has become well-known in Lean circles and is used extensively around the world as a guide to sustaining Lean in manufacturing. It turns out that sustaining Lean improvements is one of the foremost challenges of the Lean transformation in any organization. Lean is more than tools. The tools are needed, but the benefits of Lean are leveraged when it is part of the culture. In his book, David describes the team and leadership structures that are required to create and sustain Lean systems. In the office, the problem is compounded by work that remains largely invisible, embedded in computers and systems that run the business. The challenge is first knowing where and how to start, then focusing on how to take the principles of Lean and apply them to the office areas, and then later on how to sustain the gains and make them part of the culture across the enterprise.

The story begins in 1996. We were on a journey of embedding Lean into manufacturing at Steelcase, a global leader in the sales and manufacturing of office systems and environments. The products encompass tables, chairs, desks, panel systems, architectural walls, lighting, and all of the products needed to outfit an entire office floor. Steelcase had been in the office furniture business since 1912, but the challenges of running a manufacturing business were mounting. In 1996, the competition from abroad was challenging the industry with lower cost labor in multiple global regions and making it difficult to compete on the global scale. The company was looking to transform its manufacturing systems using the Lean principles found in the Toyota Production System.

In 1996, Mark Baker was brought onboard the organization as the VP of manufacturing. With little initial experience in Lean, Mark became a remarkable student. His teachers were the internal team led by David Mann and a few occasional visits by some excellent external experts. Mark charged forward with the Lean transformation in manufacturing. He personally championed the Lean effort and spent many hours every week on the manufacturing floor looking for ways to improve flow and reduce wastes. Manufacturing leaders soon learned that if Mark came by and observed a "Lean opportunity" in their area, he would certainly follow up on his next visit and ask about the progress made. He also attended kaizen and Lean workshop report-outs every Friday. The Lean transformation occurred across all areas in the manufacturing organization and included leaders from the top to the bottom of the leadership ranks.

Over the next several years, every part of the manufacturing system was transformed. The whole operation went from a batch and queue, inventory-based model to a Lean model of continuous one-piece flow with minimal inventory. Prior to Lean, the company stored huge amounts of inventory and was very proud of its "high-rise," computerized, lights-out robotic inventory system. But keeping huge volumes of inventory was not creating the efficiencies that the organization needed to stay afloat. So, manufacturing operations were transformed to flow-based Lean systems, one value stream at a time. Steelcase reduced the manufacturing footprint from 15 million square feet to well under 5 million square feet.

The manufacturing departments also moved from paying the factory workers on a piece rate (where they were rewarded for how many parts they could make in an hour) to a team-based pay structure. This was a huge disruption to the culture of the business. Now workers were paid based on how well the overall value stream was producing products. Suppliers were brought into the transformations as well.

Many within the organization credited Lean for saving the manufacturing side of the business.

By 2001, the company was well on its way in the Lean transformation of the manufacturing systems, but then the bottom dropped out of the office furniture industry in 2002 and 2003. Shortly after the terrorist attacks on the World Trade Center and Pentagon on September 11, 2001, the economy took a terrible turn and businesses across the globe were cutting costs and reducing their capital expenditures. Across the furniture industry, business levels dropped by 45%. Suddenly, the entire company was in crisis. Luckily, thanks to Lean, manufacturing had created enough agility in the production system to quickly react to the problem, and the company was able to rapidly adjust to the unexpected downward change in volumes; however, in the rest of the business, there was nothing in place to absorb the reduction in orders.

In 2003, the leaders in the organization where searching for ideas and methods to make the office work more efficient. The business had the same amount of work but a significantly smaller workforce. Could Lean apply to the office? The leaders wondered if the application of Lean in the office would achieve dramatic results similar to those achieved in manufacturing. Just prior to this time, I had been asked to apply Lean concepts to one of the teams in the IT organization. The product data team was charged with loading the data into the order entry systems for all new products. The area was known as a huge bottleneck in the new product development value stream. So, with the help of David Mann and others in manufacturing, we took the first baby steps into the application of Lean in the office. We brought together the data team who did the work to map the current data building value stream. The team filled a wall with all of the steps in the value stream to show the many handoffs and interruptions in the work flow. A 30-foot wall of a large conference room was covered with paper and descriptions to show the data building value stream. The product data leaders and the team called the display the "wall of shame," but they left it up for several months to show the extent of the problem, and people shook their heads every time they looked at the wall and saw the complexity of the steps and the obvious wastes in the data building value stream. The wall also launched a number of improvement kaizens, which began the transformation. The wall became a constant reminder of both the need for Lean transformation and tracking the improvements in the value stream. Both the wall and the improvement plans were shared with senior corporate leaders.

The conclusion by the senior leaders from this early experiment was that the company could and should try to implement Lean in the office. The organization had been very successful in modeling the Toyota Production System in the factory; why not apply what had been learned about Lean there and apply it to the office? But, how would one apply Lean concepts from manufacturing in the office? This was uncharted territory. Transferring the Lean concepts from manufacturing to the office was difficult to imagine and a little bit like trying to translate one language into some second, previously unknown, language. It's difficult to translate anything from one language to another, but with Lean there are also so many concepts and words that have no equivalent words in the new language. In this case, the two languages (Lean in manufacturing versus Lean the office) had tremendous cultural differences and very different types of work. This was compounded by many in the office who held the attitude that Lean would never work in the office. The task of translating Lean manufacturing to the office was daunting.

Yet, Jim Hackett, the CEO at the time, and the other senior leaders believed that all of the work that had been accomplished in manufacturing to implement Lean principles would have similar results in the office, and the leadership made a commitment to implement them. Suddenly the concept of a *Lean Office* was not an academic effort anymore. We had to do this. So, David Mann was moved from manufacturing to head up a Lean initiative in the office. He assembled a small team, and we started studying and experimenting with Lean principles and tools in the office. Fortunately for Steelcase, we also received great teaching and coaching from outside the company from Drew Locher. He became our chief interpreter, helping us map terminology and techniques from the foreign cultures of manufacturing into the office.

At the time, Drew Locher and John Shook had been working with General Motors on Lean office infinitives. GM had said, "we don't know if it will work in the office, but we want to figure it out." They discovered that Lean principles and techniques did translate to the office, and there were tremendous untapped opportunities for improvement! Better yet, GM was willing to share their learning with Steelcase.

One of the early "go-n-see" field trips the Steelcase team took was to GM to learn their basic approach of applying value stream mapping to an office work flow. David Mann loaded the van with the newly formed Lean office team and drove to the GM headquarters in Detroit, Michigan. I still remember driving the large Steelcase blue van from Grand Rapids to Detroit, with row seats loaded with the new Office Lean Team, and how the van barely fit into the GM parking structure. The team was filled with expectation. Once inside the building, we entered a large room that housed the artifacts of the Lean projects they were working on. They pulled out huge panels on wheels. Each one documented a different office value stream map, including the many kaizen improvements required to transform the flow of work and information. On this trip, we learned the basic approach of applying value stream mapping techniques in the office. We also learned the model of including leaders in the transformation process to help pave the way for change and remove any roadblocks and barriers.

The trip to GM was pivotal in the definition of the program, and we learned a lot that helped shape our own methods and techniques. Attempting to influence and change long-standing office value streams, many of which had not changed in decades, was delicate work. We found that the beginning of each project was a critical time and had to be done correctly. We made a number of improvements to the early stages of the project, the pre-contracting, scoping, and homework.

Our team was committed to make it work. Each of us came from a different perspective and a different part of the organization. We had representation from manufacturing, finance, human resources, and engineering. In this case, the team was truly more than the sum of its parts. We soon were tackling very big and difficult problems that had plagued the organization for years. At any given time, the Office Lean Team had a dozen or more Lean projects in flight while landing others.

Before the team started, the business process value streams in the office were bogged down with wastes and delays. Information and work did not flow through the value streams. Large backlogs of work were seen across the company, and people were constantly working in fire-fighting mode putting out the latest and hottest issues. Batch processing was the norm in the office, and work didn't always flow based on customer demand. The workers got the work done, but through heroics.

The business process value streams in the office were transformed over time, project by project and department by department. Inefficient work steps were replaced by work that flowed. In many cases, the entire value stream was re-engineered to create a new and more efficient work environment. IT systems were tweaked, and in some cases they received a major overhaul to improve communication and work flow. Teams started to practice root cause thinking to correct long-standing problems. Slowly, and steadily, the vocabulary of the company changed to reflect the new Lean thinking and practices. New and foreign Lean words like value stream mapping, kaizens, heijunka, poka-yoke, obeya rooms, and A3s started to echo through the conference rooms. Unused vertical walls and even glass surfaces displayed value stream metrics, trends, and work-flow improvements. Initially, there were no office examples to look at, so we went to manufacturing to see the Lean systems being used there. However, taking Lean methods and visual boards that had tracked the flow of pieces, parts, and trim assembly and applying these methods to the information flow of the office value stream required translation and experimentation.

Value stream mapping and improvement kaizens became the mainstay practice of the Office Lean Consulting Team. We never knew exactly where the next project would take the team. The team became very diverse and knowledgeable about the office value streams and soon became a group of sought-after and trusted workshop facilitators. Each of us became known for the ability to visualize the office work on a value stream map, see the wastes, and organize the kaizens for improvements. The work requests came to the internal consulting team faster than we could handle the demand. We had created a pull for Lean office transformation. We never turned down work and soon had a growing backlog of projects and value streams. Projects were rarely pre-judged or screened based on the benefits that might be achieved. We had found early on that there were benefits in unexpected places and that by peeling back the layers of the office value streams, we would uncover opportunities for improvement.

The team did develop some key "post-project" measures that looked back over the projects just completed. The team adopted the principle that "50% of any office value stream is waste." Key improvement metrics were tracked, and benefits were logged. The benefits soon were measured in the tens of millions of dollars in year-over-year savings. We tracked the benefits for several years, but then after a time as Lean became part of the corporate culture, we stopped tracking the benefits because everyone recognized the value of office Lean, value stream mapping, and continuous improvement kaizens.

Quite early on, Lean concepts were introduced to development in both Information Technology and Product Development. I was part of that effort along with my colleague and fellow teammate, Mark Swets. We pioneered the early application of Lean in development, which included implementing learning cycles for knowledge creation, problem solving, and innovation tactics. This led to large improvements in the speed to market of major system implementation and new products. We wrote about those concepts and practices in the book *Innovative Lean Development*. The work of applying Lean methods to development has continued inside the company and has flourished. That led me to become involved with the Lean Product and Process Development Exchange (LPPDE) with some great colleagues and a 3-year stint on their Board of Directors to help advance those concepts.

At Steelcase, the evidence of Lean behavior started to appear in leaders across the company. Instead of staying in their office or merely demanding results, leaders started going on "gemba walks" to visit the places where work happens and asking how the business process value streams might be improved. The leaders enabled the transformation by allowing people time to work on continuous improvement. The key executives leading the effort took an active role in encouraging improvement initiatives going on around the company.

As training and education continued, more and more departments started practicing Lean thinking on their own. Department heads initiated their own improvement projects. Staff was hired specifically to become the Lean champions of their home departments. Idea boards started to pop up across the office, thus accelerating the positive change throughout the organization. Lean was implemented in remote offices and even through the dealer network. Lean had become embedded in the culture of the company.

As the journey continued, the Office Lean Consulting Team was distributed to work in various departments throughout the organization. Our assignments carried us to various parts of the business: information technology, the dealer network, human resources, a new division and brand for the company, and to Steelcase global business centers around the world. The work of embedding Lean into the culture continues to move forward across the company to this day.

This book covers the methods and techniques needed to orchestrate a Lean office cultural transformation and describes the Lean tools needed to change inefficient office value streams into highly efficient and optimized ones. The book will take you through the early stages of the formation of a new office Lean program, giving you the tools and techniques needed to do the same in your organization. The roles and responsibilities required to build a Lean program and culture are most likely quite dramatically different from anything your organization has attempted before. Launching the program properly is as important as the work you will do once the program is in place. This book will take you from start to the finish, from program formation to maturity. My hope is that you will rise to the pinnacle of a mature Lean culture in the office, involving the entire organization in value stream transformation and continuous improvement.

Wishing you great success in implementing a Lean culture in the office to create a delightful workplace,

Timothy Schipper

Acknowledgments

There are many people to thank for making the journey possible and helping with this book. Thanks go to David Mann, my leader during the Lean office transformation at Steelcase, who laid the groundwork and kept the team focused. David understood the behavioral aspects of changing the culture in manufacturing. However, applying Lean in the office was like sailing through unchartered waters. Very few had explored this space. Many hidden rocks and reefs needed to be avoided. David navigated the team through new waters and helped us get to the destination without sinking the boat. David encouraged us along the way, challenged us, and once in a while left us scratching our heads wondering what to do next. David was the inspiration for this book. He knew there was a story to tell.

My thanks go to my teammates, many of whom have gone on to other key roles in the organization. They made the program possible and worked together with true teamwork. Some are still at Steelcase; others are not. The original team was Debbie Moody, Ryan Schmidt, Steve Smith, Gary Tenney, and me. Mark Swets, Jon Van Sweden, Rebecca Schmidt, and Laura Wekenman later joined us. David Mann, Debbie Moody, Steve Smith, Mark Swets, Laura Wekenman, Jon Van Sweden, and I were together the longest and drove the program to perfection.

A special thanks to the early adopters in the product data department at Steelcase. John Dean, the CIO at the time, was charged with bringing a silo-ed and fractured part of the organization into a cohesive whole. He brought me into early planning sessions with the product data leadership team. The newly appointed director, Chuck Walker, became a true believer in the power of Lean and recognized the need to make it part of the culture of the newly formed organization that had brought many functions into one department. Chuck became a chief promoter in IT and a spokesman for Lean around the company. He preached the benefits of bringing Lean concepts to the office. Doug Benner, who worked for Chuck at the time, was also a key supporter and part of the earliest experiments of forming Lean flow work cells in the office. Doug was part of all of the initiatives in the area and to this day remains a champion of the Lean transformation. Doug, now the leader of this part of the organization, is always part of customer and benchmark visits to Steelcase. Doug does an outstanding job of showcasing the progress made from implementing Lean practices.

Much appreciation needs to go out to the many others in the organization who support Lean initiatives. Some are still in the organization, and others have retired or continued their careers in other places. Their examples and case studies appear in this book.

We also could never have achieved the progress or momentum without key leaders within the organization. The first Lean action committee was made up of our key executives: Frank Merlotti Jr., our president who was a true champion; Nancy Hickey, the VP of Human Resources who believed that Lean was an important endeavor for the organization; Mark Baker, the VP of manufacturing who was a champion from day one; and Jim Keane (at that time our CFO and now the CEO of Steelcase) who recognized the tremendous benefits that Lean would bring to the organization. This group was pivotal in getting the program started and forming the team mentioned above. A special thanks to Jim Hackett, our CEO at the time, who really believed that Lean was a key initiative in transforming the business process value streams. He was an advocate and supporter of the initiative from the beginning and throughout the initiative.

This book is not only about the Lean transformation at Steelcase. Others have decided to explore this uncharted ocean, leaving the dock of safety to try new methods. Some of their stories are in these pages as well. They have investigated how to create a Lean culture and make it part of their own way of doing business. A special thanks goes out to those who reviewed the case studies and edited the content of the book, including Doug Benner and Audra Hartges for Steelcase, Brandyn Deckinga and Luke Ferris of Habitat for Humanity of Kent County, Angie Barksdale for West MichiganWorks!, Deidre Honner and Lucas Moore of Calvin College, Rich Sheridan of Menlo Innovations, and Tracy Brower of Steelcase.

My hope is that you and your team join me on this great Lean adventure of transforming the culture inside your organization. The goal in my mind is to make our places of work efficient and more joyful environments where there is *no wasteful work*. Toyota teaches that we are not respecting our employees and co-workers when there is wasteful work in the value stream. The goal is to continually remove wastes. I hope that your work culture becomes a place that practices continuous improvement and respect for people. In the Toyota Lean culture, the pillars don't define the culture; they just describe the tools and practices to get to a Lean culture. You will have to define the Lean culture for your organization. My desire is that this book will help you learn from others who have gone before you. My mission is to help organizations achieve a delightful office culture by transforming their business process value streams, removing wastes, and making continuous improvements.

The greatest thanks go to my wife Karen and our family, who have been supportive of my work in the area of Lean and listened to my Lean stories with interest. They have encouraged me at every step, and when David suggested that I write this book, my wife told me to "go for it." I am very grateful to my family, a constant source of encouragement and love.

About the Author

 **Timothy Schipper** is a graduate of Calvin College and the University of Michigan (Bachelor's of Mechanical Engineering and Master's of Science). His career has spanned 30 years and includes time as a tool designer, engineering educator, CAD specialist, senior product engineer, IT manager, and Lean expert, author, coach, and consultant. His teaching experience includes positions in the Engineering Department at Calvin College and in industry. He has led Lean transformations in the areas of office value streams, IT development, product development, new business initiatives, government agencies, and nonprofits.

He currently works for Steelcase Inc. of Grand Rapids, Michigan, where he coaches leadership and teams in the areas of Lean product design, Lean management systems, and business transformations. He is the founder of Lean Inspiration, which promotes Lean concepts to organizations and non-profits through writing, educational classes, coaching, and workshops.

Timothy served for 3 years as an officer on the Board of Directors of LPPDE, Inc., an international nonprofit group that promotes the exchange ideas and practices used in Lean development. Timothy is the co-author of *Innovative Lean Development: How to Create, Implement, and Maintain a Learning Culture*, Schipper & Swets, Productivity Press © 2010, which explores how rapid learning cycles, knowledge management, and other Lean techniques can be applied in development. He has also written articles in *AME Target Magazine*, in Wikipedia ("Design for Lean Manufacturing"), and he has contributed material for other authors (Steve Bell, Katherine Radeka, and Durward Sobek). He speaks at North American and international conferences on the topics of Lean, innovation, and leadership. You can follow him on Twitter (@LeanInspirations) or on his blog (http://innovativeLean.wordpress.com).

Section I

The Lean Office

1

Lean Culture in the Office

"BEHAVIORS PRACTICED OVER TIME BECOME CULTURE"

Nearly every office around the world is missing a critical practice that would greatly increase the efficiency of the workers and improve its processes. The workers live and work in a broken system or in some cases work without a system at all. As Deming so aptly told us, "A bad system will beat a good person every time." People working in broken systems are demoralized and often lack motivation to perform. Even though wastes are being eliminated daily from the manufacturing of products, and the parts and assembly process flow are dramatically improved through the application of continuous improvement and the application of Lean tools, just over the concrete walls in the carpeted areas of the office realm, there are wastes and inefficiencies that would greatly benefit from the same practice of continuous improvement that is used to transform the production side of the business.

The concepts of Lean are easy to understand and grasp, but transferring them from manufacturing to the office is a difficult task. There is a feeling of resistance to tools that work in manufacturing but "would never work here in the office." This book spells out methods for taking Lean methods that have been widely practiced in manufacturing and how to apply them to the carpeted office areas of the organization. In these pages, the methods for making Lean part of the culture across the enterprise are explored and explained. Any office value stream from the corporate boardroom to the mailroom can benefit from the application of Lean principles. A Lean culture of continuous improvement can be fostered, and gains from implemented ideas can yield tremendous benefits in the office and administrative areas. Lean can help find the wastes and transform the office value streams that cross organizational boundaries. The missing critical practice is the practice of continuous improvement.

There are three pillars for the application of Lean in the office. These are the core of transforming the office value streams.

1. Lean tools are applied to recognize and remove wastes from the value streams in the organization.
2. Improvements are made to improve the value streams that cross organizational boundaries.
3. Lean behaviors become part of the Lean culture through employee involvement and sharing.

Chapter 2 looks at the first pillar and teaches how to find and recognize wastes in office value streams. Chapters 3 and 4 describe how to lay the groundwork in the organization to start a Lean journey. Chapters 5 through 7 examine how to tackle value stream improvement projects. Sprinkled throughout the book, and focused in depth in the final chapters, are the topics of Lean behaviors for cultural transformation, described and demonstrated with the use of examples and case studies. Each chapter ends with the one main thing, the key takeaway from the content, and a set of study questions to be used to bring Lean thinking to the office and administrative areas inside your organization.

INTRODUCTION TO WASTES

The term "wastes" in office Lean refers to any and all activities that do not add value for the customer. Wastes lead to delays and defects of the delivery of information and services in the office value streams. These wastes create lost productivity and often result in errors that require rework. Chapter 2 describes the wastes commonly found in office value streams and discusses some ways to eliminate them. The application of Lean in the office seeks to find the wastes and eliminate their root causes from the work steps in the office.

Administrative systems in the office typically suffer from years of neglect and a lack of attention, which produce inefficiencies and wastes. The wastes are not intended; they simply enter the system over time. People in the office are trying to compensate for things that don't work. When approaching office work and applying Lean thinking, you can start with the assumption that up to 50% of the administrative value streams are filled with wasteful work. Wherever there are handoffs, assume that 50% can be removed. Where wait time exists, it can be improved by 50%. Redundant steps can be eliminated. Some have estimated that as much as 90% of the work in an office value stream is wasteful and that many of the things done by the workers do not add any value for the customer. By applying Lean techniques, an organization can eliminate those wastes.

INTRODUCTION TO VALUE STREAMS IN THE OFFICE

Much of the book is devoted to methods to improve the value stream in the office. A value stream is an end-to-end system that serves the customer or the users of the services that are provided by the organization. A value stream consists of all of the process steps from beginning to end. In manufacturing, the output of the value streams in the plant is the product produced in the plant. In the office however, the value streams are defined by the information that is provided or the service that is being performed. There are usually several main value streams in the organization. Here are some common office value streams:

- Concepts to development of new products or services
- Sales for new and existing clients
- Ordering to delivery of products or services
- Order to payment for services (often called order to cash)
- Customer service value stream
- Procuring goods and materials to support the organization

The application of Lean in the office involves understanding and improving the value streams and all of the sub-level value streams and steps that make up the larger value stream. Unfortunately, the high-level value streams are often so complex that they must be broken down in smaller parts to tackle their complexity. Any value stream can be mapped and described with a simple set of value stream mapping symbols. Once the current condition (what we will call the current state) of the value stream is visually mapped and understood, an improved future state is created to help direct the activities that will improve it. This formula will be utilized over and over again in the organization to find the problems and wastes in the value stream and systematically remove them.

Step 1: Map the current state of the value stream.
Step 2: Identify the wastes in the value stream.
Step 3: Envision the future state of the value stream.
Step 4: Map out the improvement activities to improve it.

INTRODUCTION TO A CULTURE OF CONTINUOUS IMPROVEMENT

The goal of Lean is to create a culture of continuous improvement in the organization, and it seeks to involve everyone in the organization in making positive changes on a daily basis. Efficiency can be improved anywhere inside the organization by applying Lean thinking, which involves practicing and applying a series of repeatable tools and techniques. The Lean culture is evident when everyone in the organization is practicing Lean thinking and making continuous improvements to the value stream. Building a Lean culture includes everybody in the organization, from the leaders to the receptionist, from the managers to the front-line staff. Everyone is trained and attuned to seeing the wastes and eliminating them.

A focus on continuous improvement is not a normal activity in most organizations, which are usually focused on results and addressing the latest crisis. In most organizations, people are working on the latest fire of the day. They are busy tackling the latest emergency, or they are scrambling to address the latest customer complaint. In this environment of constantly addressing things that need urgent attention throughout the day, the morale of the people can become very low. And in the fire-fighting culture, things are fixed by heroics. Heroics can cause people to turn a "blind eye" to the problems in the value stream. Results are achieved, but the broken value streams in the office are only temporarily fixed to achieve those results. Since people are living in a whirlwind of daily activity and pressure to obtain results, no one within the organization, at any level, feels comfortable or fulfilled in the fire-fighting, results-driven culture, except the firefighters!

What is a Lean Culture?

The challenge is to rise above the demoralizing environment of fire-fighting behavior and to transform the organization into one focused on continuous improvement of the value streams. In the Lean culture, the goal is for everyone in the organization to be working toward getting out of the whirlwind of fire fighting and the heroics that go along with it. Leadership must stop rewarding heroics and train and encourage all of the staff to make improvements. The staff will then be inspired to remove the wastes and being to think of ways to prevent them from happening over and over again. Over time, the staff sees that the new environment is much better, more efficient, and less stressful. A Lean culture is one in which everybody recognizes problems on a daily basis and seeks to put ideas in place to fix them. There are ideas and improvements made every day.

David Mann, PhD in industrial psychology, my mentor and sensei, points out in *Creating a Lean Culture* that this new culture is not a construct or destination in itself. While it is a goal, it is not the target. That is to say, it is not achievable or measurable on its own. Mann notes that culture, by itself, is a hypothetical construct. The culture can be loosely described by how it feels or looks, but that doesn't allow us to understand or create it. You can see the evidence of culture, but it is difficult to create.

What is the target then, if it is not the culture? While a culture of Lean in the office might be recognized through evidence of continuous improvement, waste elimination to create efficiencies, and problem solving, those are not the goals. The goals are the behaviors, practices, and even the habits that create a Lean culture of continuous improvement.

Cultural Change is driven by:

- Changes in behavior
- New practices performed on a regular basis
- Consistent practices reinforced with new habits

The understanding that culture needs new behaviors, practices, and habits allows us to understand why it is so difficult to achieve. Everyone knows that it is difficult to change a habit. Losing weight is difficult because it requires what we call a "life-style change." To lose weight, a person must change diet and daily activity levels through exercise. The old habit of reaching for the donut or cookie has to be replaced with a new habit of reaching for carrot and celery sticks and replacing mash potatoes and gravy with vegetables and fruit. Sitting in front of the television or at our desks all day has to be replaced with movement and exercise.

Lean is a term and concept used to describe a way of thinking about and acting on the organization's value streams so that they are constantly improving, and Lean can be applied to the office and administrative systems just as easily as it has been applied in manufacturing. The word "Lean" was first introduced by Jim Womack and a graduate student at MIT, and the word was selected to communicate the efficiency they saw after studying Japanese companies like Toyota (*The Machine That Changed the World*). Just as an athlete has the discipline to train daily toward a goal, Lean organizations build discipline by continually moving toward becoming more efficient. If we want a new culture, we have to change the underlying practices and habits that define the current culture. We need people to exercise new behaviors on a regular, daily basis.

Throughout the book, the principles of Lean for the office will be explored. The principles are the practices and behaviors that are practiced over and over again to improve the systems and value streams of the organization.

These 10 principles are the focus of the leadership and employees in a Lean organization. They are the practices that are embedded in the Lean organization. Overtime, they become common practices and habits. They are constantly taught and referred to and often prominently displayed inside the organization. Lean companies are not bashful about making the principles part of their public-facing statements about who they are and how they work.

RESPECT FOR OFFICE WORKERS

A culture of Lean starts with people. People come first in a Lean company. I once heard a Lean coach from Toyota describe respect for people this way, "If there is wasteful work in the system, then the leadership is not respecting the people." This means we need to remove any waste in the office value streams that makes work more difficult for the employees. When you have a wasteful office value stream, you are disrespecting your customers and the employees within the organization. If there are inefficiencies, and people are expected to struggle and work heroics to get things done, then the staff is not respected. Dr. Deming said,

TABLE 1.1

Lean Principles and Practices

Lean Principles	The Lean Practices
Make the work flow	• Work toward the flow of information across the value streams. • Avoid delays, interrupters. • Start tasks and finish them. • Avoid multitasking. • Check the status at regular intervals.
See customer value	• Give value to the end customer. • Avoid any unnecessary trouble for the end customer. Describe value from the point of view of the customer. Eliminate non-value-added activities.
Eliminate wastes	• Develop "eyes for wastes." • Work to see the wastes in the value streams. • Eliminate the wastes. • Seek to prevent them from re-occurring.
Continuous improvement	• View Lean as a journey. • Always seek to identify and fix problems. • Don't be satisfied with the current situation. • Always work toward the next future state. • Never stop improving.
Accountability for improvement	• Get everyone involved. • Establish accountability for making improvements.
Standardize the value stream	• Create standards for work. • Follow the standards. • Continually improve the steps. • Regularly refine the standard work practices.
Visual controls	• Use vertical surfaces or whiteboards to display the current state of the value stream. • Display improvements. • Share continuous improvement.
Quality at the source	• Ensure that the work is complete and accurate at every step. • Do not pass problems, issues, or missing information on to the next step. • Perform inspections before passing work on to the next person in the chain.
Measure the value stream	• Remember that what gets measured gets done. Measure the value stream (not the people).

(*Continued*)

TABLE 1.1 (Cont.)

Lean Principles	The Lean Practices
	• Make the measures visible and the work methods transparent. • Use measures to drive improvements to the value stream.
Leadership involvement	• Leaders practice Lean principles. • Leaders are the teachers and coaches. • Leaders set the Lean vision in their areas. • Leaders set aside time in the organization for continuous improvement activities.

"A bad system will beat good people every time." The new practice in Lean is to eliminate the bad systems instead of simply enduring their inefficiencies. In the Lean office, all members of the staff are involved in and contribute to improvements. If the bad systems are left in place, then we are asking the people in the organization to compensate, work heroics, and live in a sea of wastes. In Lean, we ask the people in the organization to work toward eliminating the wastes. Additionally, if you pass waste on to the end customers or end users, then they are not respected because they are not getting the full value from the product or service that your organization is delivering.

Respect for people means that the organization will

- provide training and coaching for people on how to improve their own value streams,
- give them time to make improvements,
- think across the value stream and build partnerships between departments and with suppliers,
- learn to see the wastes and remove them,
- avoid the mindset that things will get better on their own, and
- assume that all areas in a value stream need improvement.

Doing these things will create a delightful experience in the office.
May the Force be With You:

A dark side to Lean has to be faced head on. Will Lean reduce wastes and remove cost from the organization? Yes, it will. Will Lean increase the efficiency of the workers in the office? Yes, it will. Will practicing Lean free up the time of office workers? Yes, it will. However, cost cutting and staff reductions are not the goal of a Lean program. Creating a competitive advantage and efficiency in an increasingly competitive environment is the goal of Lean.

I always get a question in classes from people who are new to Lean and associate Lean with cost-cutting measures or reductions of force. I give a few simple answers to this:

1. The management team has to be clear that Lean is an improvement system and not a cost-cutting activity. In fact, the leadership team that has to say, "No one will lose his or her job because of Lean." Furthermore, if office workers anticipate that the leadership team is introducing the Lean initiative to cut costs and reduce people, they will quickly reject the whole notion.
2. If there is a need to reduce the workforce due to economic conditions, then the recommendation is to be clear about why, and the leadership team should make the reductions before they start a Lean program.
3. Workers need to be allowed to move freely in the organization and will need to be trained for new jobs. Lean will bring more efficiency to some parts of the organization than others, which will free up workers, and people will need to be retrained and allowed to transfer to other areas of the organization. Leadership needs to support the retraining and movement of people.

Now for the bright side of Lean: Once the skills of Lean are learned and practiced, Lean can be simple and fun. The tools for improvement are easily understood and easy to apply. A true sensei breaks down the skills of difficult routines and makes them appear smooth and seamless to the student. Similarly, in Lean, the skills of breaking down value streams and removing wastes can be systematically transferred to the people in the organization. Learning Lean requires learning and applying Lean methods that will remove the wastes from the value stream. With a little training and ongoing encouragement, the workers will discover that they can change the system. A best practice in Lean is to develop the people and to teach them how to remove waste from their own value stream. People are most satisfied when they are empowered and have control of their work. Lean seeks to turn the keys over to the staff so that they can make their own improvements which makes work more purposeful and meaningful for them.

WHERE TO START? MAKE IT VISUAL

The visual tools in Lean help to make the value stream better and more transparent; they put the team on the path of improvement. Value stream measures are made visible, which seek to measure the current condition of the value stream to understand how the systems are performing right now. Lean metrics are not "rear view mirror" business reports and updates focused on the performance of the organization for the last month or quarter. Most reports and internal metrics are done by looking at past performance. While those metrics are important for understanding and measuring the success of an organization, they do not help drive continuous improvement. The backward-looking metrics are important to the Board of Directors and leaders for looking in the rear-view mirror before setting a new direction and strategy.

Lean measures are different.

Lean metrics focus on the improvement efforts going on in the business each day: the amount of improvement, the pace of improvement, and the degree of involvement of the whole organization, etc. Lean metrics focus on the health of the value stream. How is the value stream performing today? Are we ahead or behind? Can the team handle the next spike in demand? Lean also measures the elements of Lean culture including leadership buy-in, employee involvement, evidence of reaching the improvement goals, and ultimately whether value is improving for the customer.

The Lean measures are made visible and are intended to make the value stream transparent. The measures that are displayed on the visual board throughout the office need to show how things are running today. The metrics take on many forms, and the chapter on visual controls will show a number of examples.

When work is made visible, everyone in the organization knows where things stand. No one is kept in the dark. If the leader needs to answer a question about the status of work, he or she simply goes to the visual wall to check on the status of the work.

The first Lean implementation at a team level.

1. Display a metric measuring the current status of the value stream.
2. Put up an improvement board and assign tasks for improvement.
3. Hold daily improvement meetings.
4. Leaders empower and support the team.

The team will use the visual board that displays the metric and use it as the location for the team's daily stand-up meeting. At the board, the team talks about the improvements that are being made to the value stream. Every person on the team gets involved in making improvements to the value stream. As ideas for improvements are suggested in the daily stand-up meeting, the team records those and assigns ownership. The daily stand-up meeting becomes one of the most important meetings of the day. The team gathers around the visuals for a short meeting to discuss the current status of the work and what improvements could be made. Stand-up meetings are short 15-minute meetings, and they are typically done by gathering around the team's visual board (see Figure 1.1).

Stand-up meetings happen in the office, just as they do in the plant. There is space reserved for displaying visuals. An entire area in the plant is sectioned off for the purpose of showing the visuals. In the office, a conference room with whiteboards is used for visuals. The team gathers at least once per day around the visuals to check on the current

FIGURE 1.1
Stand-up meeting – 15 minutes every day to report on status and improvements.

status of the value stream. They discuss issues with the work and highlight the interrupters that prevent work from happening.

The team members cover three points in the stand-up meeting:

1. What is the current status of the value stream?
2. What is preventing work from getting done (what are the wastes)?
3. How can I help?

In the same meeting, people are looking for ways to improve the systems and work methods.

What ideas are there for improving the value stream?
What improvements have been made that we can share?

When the team hears that everyone is concerned about the process steps and offering to help each other, the morale of the team is greatly improved. And when workers see that their teammates are working on ways to improve the value stream, they feel empowered to do the same.

All office work can be improved, and looking for wastes, and being aware of possible improvements, is something that everyone can do. At first, the team needs to be taught and coached on how to see the wastes. They also have to be assured that the stand-up meeting is a safe zone for reporting on wastes. No finger pointing allowed. The Lean perspective is that a breakdown of the value stream causes the problems, not the people. It has been my experience that 99.9% of the time, people want to do a good job and complete the work. The systems are causing the problems, not the people. Out of each stand-up meeting, there should be clear ownership by the person who will take action against the waste. Each meeting has a time for reporting on who is working on which waste problem. In Lean, we call this accountability for improvement.

The team's focus is on removing the wastes from the value stream. As the team talks about the current status of the work moving through the process steps, the team members are taking time to think about how each step needs to change. The daily focus is on the waste in the system. If the job was completed in 3 days, the team asks how it can be completed in 2 days. If the same errors are repeated, the team asks how they can be removed from the systems. If work is delayed, then the team asks how to improve the value stream and remove the delays. The team is constantly challenging everything about the systems.

Making It Fun

The team's involvement in improving the work is inspiring for the team. The work is no longer the enemy because the team is working toward understanding what should change to make it better. Lean gives the team new ways to think about the how the work gets done. This removes the challenges and barriers. Lean can simplify the work and make the work more fun. The team is working on these changes all day long and makes this part of the way they think about their work. They're always looking for ways to identify waste and to remove the wastes. The daily stand-up meeting becomes the checkpoint at the beginning of each day when the team can share its progress in improving the value stream, or someone may simply share a challenge or problem and ask teammates for help in improving the systems used to get the work done. The daily state of meaning becomes one of the events in the daily routine into supply of the team.

The daily stand-up meaning is also the time when the team can share the improvements that have been made. A world-class Lean company tracks ideas that are implemented at the team level (Robinson and Schroeder). In chapter 10 of this book on the mature Lean organization, the details of how to create a functioning idea system in the office will be explored. However, at this point, the emphasis is on the importance of all employees working on implementing ideas inside of the organization. World-class companies develop cultures of nearly 100% participation in generating and implementing ideas, and each employee generates up to 100 ideas (implemented) every year. Some ideas are larger and more impactful, but no idea is too small to be considered. The small ideas help to build momentum inside the organization and move the culture toward Lean. Many small changes over time can add up to significant gains. In reality, it is unclear at first glance how much some ideas might improve the work methods inside the organization. Employee involvement in the continuous improvement cycle is the evidence of a Lean culture. Having this level of continuous improvement is exciting and inspiring. Employee-led improvements will drive the organization to become more fit and efficient.

Leader Behavior

The organizational structure of a Lean company or organization may not look that much different from outside the four walls of the company. The difference comes in the practices, behaviors, and habits that the team and the leaders practice every day. There is a difference in how the leaders investing their time and energy.

The leadership team in the office creates the environment for Lean to prosper. Many of the Lean behaviors will seem foreign to the staff, and in fact, the staff may be practicing the exact opposite behavior. The leadership has to provide coaching and create a safe environment for Lean behaviors. The safe environment is one in which it is perfectly okay to raise issues, talk about performance misses, and discuss problems without pointing fingers. In a Lean environment, value streams and their status are displayed visually, and if a value stream is not healthy, that condition will be shown visually. In fact, the status will be given a red dot on the visual board. The red dot can apply to a metric, a project, an initiative, or any action item displayed on the visual board. The first time red appears in a prominent place in the office, leadership and teams will become very nervous. The leader's job is to reassure direct reports that red shows the true status of the work. The leader will have to reassure other leaders and the staff over and over again: "It is okay to show red, because we want to expose problems so that they can be fixed. Red is not the fault of the person in the value stream, and we do not point fingers. Red is a chance to help a fellow coworker."

This type of safe environment of exposing problems is practiced inside of Toyota, and it has been described as "The Culture of Red." The culture of red is one in which it is acceptable and commonplace to discuss issues and problems. These types of Lean behaviors are described in Table 1.2 and contrasted with the typical "non-Lean' behaviors. It is also a place where coworkers jump in to help when something needs fixing or improvement due to increased demand.

TABLE 1.2

The Lean Behaviors

Lean	Not Lean
Focused on the value stream	Focused on results
"Improve the work"	"Get the work done"
Make improvements everyday	Limited or no time for improvement
Make the work visual	Work is hidden from view
Work standards constantly updated	Work standards are stagnant
Create a safe environment	Finger pointing
Fire prevention	Fire fighting
Negative results are visible	Negative results are hidden
Problems are exposed	Problems are buried

The Lean leader and Lean staff are always trying to shift to the behaviors in the left column. I will talk about making work visual throughout the book. For now, I will just state that the purpose of the visuals in the office is to move from hidden processes and unknown status of work to visible work and known status all the time. Visuals in a Lean organization are used to make hidden steps visible, so that everybody can check to see if the value stream is healthy.

Visuals should highlight misses and point to problems.

The leaders are committed to looking at problems and issues and removing wastes from the organization. The leaders ask different questions. The leaders ask

- Is the customer value improving?
- Are we measuring the right things?
- Are things improving?
- Is everyone on my team involved in continuous improvement?
- How can I as the leader help them and remove roadblocks?

So, every part of the leader's day has some element focused on eliminating waste and activities to improve the value streams in the office. The leader's mission does not have an end date. Once leaders are on the path of continuous improvement, they never deviate from the path. It becomes part of the fabric of the organization. Here's the caveat: if only the leader practices seeing and removing wastes, and the team is not involved, the culture has not yet been transformed. The leader can demonstrate the behavior but also needs to encourage the behavior in the people.

Daily Improvement Stand-Up Meetings

The leader will also change the management of accountability surrounding improvements. The Lean leader puts a tracking system in place that enables the team to track the improvements that have been made. This can be a simple system of team names and sticky notes. Figure 1.2 shows a simple visual board that can be used to track improvements. The sticky notes show what improvement work is being done by each team member. A small white board is all that is needed for a visual display like this. The beauty is that any team can do this for a very small investment in money and time.

FIGURE 1.2
A simple Lean improvement board in the office.

The Lean leader will look at more than whether work got done?" This leader will also regularly ask, "Are people improving the systems?" The improvement system, or commitment system, also looks for evidence that the value stream follows repeatable standards. Action items to improve in these areas are tracked. The leader will be looking for deviations from those standards as an indicator that the staff is not following the appropriate process steps, and deviations might cause a problem.

Some think that Lean is opposed to innovation because it focuses on standards and standard work. This incorrect perception might come from witnessing that a worker followed the standard work and was reluctant to change it. Workers who are unwilling to change the process steps are focused too much on sticking to the work standards and not enough on continually improving the work.

Lean is Meant to be a Structured Method for Workers to Change Their Own Value Stream

The intent of Lean is to constantly improve the value stream by empowering any person in the system to think about how the work should change and get better. Having stable work standards that don't change is not the goal. In fact, work standards should be constantly changing. Work standards should be made so they are simple to change, and they should change frequently. Work standards and procedures that are visual in nature are the easiest to maintain.

The purpose of the regular improvement meetings is to encourage a culture in which every person is generating ideas that eliminate wastes. The motto "no wasteful work" becomes the rally cry for the team.

Leadership's Role in Creating a Lean Culture

A successful Lean culture requires a passionate leader who believes that Lean will truly make a difference in the organization. Showing value stream status or highlighting problems by showing them on a visual wall can be very uncomfortable in many organizations. The leader has to set an atmosphere that ensures there is no finger pointing, and he or she will emphasize that the purpose of showing problems is to generate ideas and develop solutions to fix them.

In the culture of continuous improvement, the leader assigns some amount of time for improvement. This might be the start of the day, carved out at the end of the day, or be another designated time. The idea is that some time is reserved for all employees to make incremental small improvements. People often ask me how much time a team should devote to continuous improvement.

- Devote 5 to 10% of your week to continuous improvement, 2 to 4 hours of a 40-hour work week
- Ideally, set a time aside for the team to discuss and make improvements together.

When you look at setting aside a small amount of time for Lean, there is less of an argument that "I don't have time for continuous improvement." Most of us easily lose 20 minutes of time during our days in wastes anyway. The goal is to convert some of the idle time to eliminating waste.

Later in the book, we will look at a workshop model to improve the value stream that requires a little more investment of time from Lean leaders and office workers alike. However, even in the workshop model the goal is to limit the time it absorbs. Office workers are usually very,

very busy. Many times, each is the only one doing a specific job. This means that you can't pull people away from their work for long periods of time. By setting a goal of devoting a small about of time to continuous improvement, everyone can participate.

The senior leader sets the atmosphere of the Lean program inside the organization. To achieve cultural changes in practices and behaviors, the leader will need the assistance of change agents inside the organization. These change agents are the Lean leaders, and they are appointed by the senior leader to ensure the success of the program.

The Lean leaders need to be people who are respected inside of the organization. They often will need to lead by influence, rather than by positional authority. They will be working across the value streams inside the organization. Since they will be working on the value streams that cross functional departments, the leader requires a high degree of respect across the organization.

Lean leaders become the evangelists for Lean inside of the organization. Depending on the size of the organization, the leadership might appoint a central team of Lean leaders. Individual departments may also desire their own Lean leaders. The leader role can be full or part time. If the role is part time, then the senior leader needs to free up enough time (50% is a recommendation) from the leader's responsibilities to allow sufficient focus on Lean.

The Lean leader's role is to help teach and coach the teams. While the topics of Lean are simple to use, creating change within the organization is not easy. The specific job duties of the Lean leader are to

- be a student of Lean,
- teach Lean practices,
- demonstrate Lean behavior,
- facilitate Lean workshops,
- coach teams with improvement events,
- facilitate root cause and corrective action problem solving sessions, and
- assist the teams with their idea systems.

The Lean leader should become a constant student of Lean: reading books about Lean, attending Lean conferences, listening to podcasts, etc., learning Lean to apply it to the work environment and daily life. The Lean leader will also develop a network within the organization, and outside the organization, with other Lean leaders and experts. He or she is constantly building a skillset to can help the organization implement the concepts.

The leaders are the go-to people for Lean advice. They help to teach the basics of Lean to the staff. They also facilitate Lean workshops and problem-solving sessions. The leader takes the participants on a step-by-step journey from the land of wastes to a new promised land where the wastes are eliminated and the value streams are improved. In Part II of this book, we will go in depth into the Lean workshop model. The leader knows what areas not to visit, what to go through quickly, and where to spend more time. The workshop model is one area on which the Lean leader spends a lot of time. The other is in daily problem solving and idea generation and implementation.

Since much of the Lean culture is driven by staff attention to solving problems, the Lean leader facilitates and guides the staff in making the behaviors of waste identification and process improvement part of the culture. The leader helps the team understand the techniques in getting to the true root cause of the problems and will facilitate sessions with the team to help identify a problem and then break it down to find the root cause. The leader also helps the team think through how to apply Lean principles such as one-piece flow to the office work. The end goal is to coach the teams to do this on their own.

The leader is also working with the team to implement ideas for improvement on a daily basis. The organization that only focuses on workshops and problem solving is missing one of the key ingredients for Lean success. Employee-led ideas can represent 80% of the improvements made. If the leaders do not focus on helping the staff implement its own ideas, the organization will miss this huge opportunity. Leader-led projects and workshops represent only 20% of the Lean potential (Robinson and Schroeder, *Idea Driven Organization*). Front-line ideas generate the most benefits.

SUMMARY

The One Thing – Lean culture is about employee involvement in eliminating wastes and improving the value streams in the office with the support of the Lean leader.

STUDY QUESTIONS

1. What are the three pillars for the application of Lean in the office? What would these practices look like in your organization?
2. When approaching office work and applying Lean thinking, what percentage of the administrative value streams are filled with wasteful work?
3. What is the definition of a value stream in the office?
4. What is the formula that will be utilized over and over again in the organization to find the problems and wastes in the value stream and systematically remove them?
5. When is the Lean culture evident in the organization?
6. How does respect for people translate to Lean applied to the office?
7. What is the dark side of Lean? How is it avoided? What are the techniques to move to the bright side of Lean?
8. What is the focus of the measures in a Lean office? What are some examples of Lean measures?
9. What is one important thing to start in a value stream improvement initiative?
10. How should a leader react to the "red" condition of a value stream?
11. Why are Lean leaders so important to the Lean initiative?

2

Wastes and Why Lean Works in the Office

Wastes in office processes make work difficult and challenging. Waste results in things that bug us and cause us to redo and rework the things we have already done. We often experience the symptoms of waste without thinking about their causes. Waste resembles when we are not feeling well but do not know why. We are dealing with symptoms and treating them with whatever over-the-counter medicine we think will help. We are hoping that our self-administered medications will cure whatever it is we have. Finally, we realize that we are not getting better, so we call the doctor and go in for an appointment. The doctor asks us to describe the symptoms and runs a test or two to get to the true root cause of why we are not feeling well. The doctor diagnoses the aliment and tells us "you have such-and-such problem." At that point, our doctor can treat the disease. Wastes are a lot like symptoms that tell us we are sick, but we still have to get to their root causes.

In the office, wastes are the symptoms of a broken value stream. Identifying and exposing the wastes comprise the first step to understanding what is wrong with office value streams. The symptoms (or wastes) point to the underlying root cause. Unfortunately, value stream wastes are typically hidden from view and missing from conversations in the office.

Value stream wastes are found everywhere in the office, but you have to train your eyes to see them. The primary differences between the office and the manufacturing environment are the things we look at in each. In manufacturing, the goal is to move products through the value stream. The inventory that has built up at each process step is a clear indicator of waste. However, office value streams attempt to move information through a set of steps in a process, and information is typically hidden from plain sight. In manufacturing, the products moving through the value stream are obvious because they are physical, and the wastes can be directly observed. In contrast, office wastes are hidden from view because the information value stream takes place in the electronic systems of the organization. If you look across the office cubicles, there are busy people working but stationary, and the tasks they are performing are not visible. If there is a pattern of flow, it is unrecognizable. The process steps and the wastes need to be made visible. The wastes are used to describe the symptoms resulting in a lack of flow in the value stream. The wastes are what we are trying to minimize or remove from the value stream.

All work in the office is really a set of process steps. In fact, everything we do is a process of some type. Your morning routine is a set of processes. How you make your coffee in the morning is a process. How you load and unload the dishwasher is a process. Your drive into work is a set of steps that includes collecting the things you will need for the day, loading the car, driving to work, parking the car, unloading your stuff from the car, and walking to the building. Writing this book is a set of process steps involving collecting information, writing, editing, approving, and finally printing. How you approach the email in your inbox in the morning is a process. Taking an order at work is a process. The activities involved in making a decision are a process. Every meeting is a process. Every report or presentation you generate has a process. Lean thinkers look at the process and search for the potential wastes in the process. They then look for ways to remove the wastes.

TABLE 2.1

Lean Definitions

Lean Word	Definition
Waste	Any type of activity that slows down the work or introduces errors
Batch	Perform steps with a large set of information (usually involves waiting for the batch to be assembled or to arrive at the work step); the opposite of flow
Flow	Work is broken down into its smallest unit, and each unit is worked on in sequence, one after the other (the opposite of batch processing).
Pull	Work steps are separated by distance or departments, the priority of work is clearly defined, and the next step in the work process is chosen by priority.

Lean thinkers are removing wastes in their life every day. When a whole department or entire organization removes wastes, then the organization is building a Lean culture.

If you think of a value stream as set of process steps, you'll notice that the steps in the value stream are often words that end in "ing." These "ing" words can be the potential wastes in the value stream. Process steps in going to work can be described with "ing" words, like loading, driving, parking, unloading, and walking. As you think of any office value stream, one simple technique for waste removal is to write down all of the words that end in "ing" that represent the work steps and then attempt to reduce or remove them from the process. Sometime the entire "ing" step can be eliminated. If you think about work as a set of steps to perform a process, recognizing and removing the wastes becomes simple and easy. The words that end with "ing" form the steps that can be filled with wastes.

WASTES IN THE OFFICE

The list of wastes in Lean manufacturing originated to give a language that can be used to describe the wastes and process problems that cause a lack of flow in the factory; however, the wastes don't translate directly to the office and need to be redefined. The translation helps the organization recognize the wastes in its daily processing. In the office, just as in manufacturing, the goal is to remove the delays, handoffs, and errors that are present in the value stream. The same 8 wastes used in manufacturing are used for the office, but their meanings have to be redefined to describe the lack of flow of information and decisions through the office value stream.

The wastes are easily remembered through the mnemonic "D O W N T I M E," which is a helpful way to recall them when diagnosing value stream wastes. The wastes are easily memorized, and once you have them in your head, you will start to see them everywhere. When we look at the wastes in Table 2.2, personal examples immediately start to jump out. We start recalling situations when these wastes have been experienced. Actually, the wastes appear everywhere in the processing of information in the office, and we will notice wastes at home as well. A great exercise is to take one value stream and try to list as many wastes in the process steps as possible. After listing the wastes, next determine what could be done to eliminate or reduce each one. The earmark of a Lean culture is that the leaders and the

TABLE 2.2

Wastes Defined for the Office

Waste	Definition for the Office	Examples of Office Wastes
Defects	Information that is missing or in error; anything in the office that has to be redone or reworked and sent back to the requestor for clarification or correction	• Errors in documents • Incorrect data entries • Wrong information that is shared • Forwarding incomplete documents or emails
Over-production (Over-doing)	Creating information before it is needed or creating more than is needed by the customer or others in the process	• Printing or sending information even when it is not required • Making extra copies • Creating reports no one reads
Waiting	Waiting for information or decisions	• Bottlenecks • Ineffective meetings • Waiting for approvals • System downtime
Non-utilized resources	Any underutilized resources of people, computers, office space, or equipment	• Limited authority to make decisions • Not delegating • Lack of cross-training of people • Incorrect people assigned to a job or task • Only one person does the job, no back-up • Unused supplies, equipment, computers, or printers
Transportation	Movement of people or information by "wings or wheels"; movement of documents, supplies, or people by planes, cars, trucks, mail trucks, etc.	• Movement of files • Driving or flying to meetings without need • Physical mail, courier services, or inter-office transfers
Inventory	Any piece of work or information that is sitting without activity; this includes email inboxes, workflows, lines, and physical files and documents	• Physical or computer files • Email inboxes not zeroed out everyday • Printed materials

(*Continued*)

TABLE 2.2 (Cont.)

Waste	Definition for the Office	Examples of Office Wastes
Motion	Excess motion in the workplace of people or information; this includes any handoffs or back and forth movement of information.	• Looking for items in inventory • Looking for supplies • Walking to and from the printer/copier • Finding lost files or items
Extra-processing	Doing more than is needed by the customer, the downstream process, or the workers receiving the work	• Saving multiple copies in different locations • The same data required and duplicated in different places • Follow-ups to find answers • Unneeded approvals or signatures

staff are relentless about identifying and eliminating wastes from the office value streams. If the organization is systematically eliminating wastes, it is practicing the behavior to build a Lean culture.

For example, take a look at the extra inventory, waiting, excess motion, and extra-processing of your own email inbox value stream. The email that has stalled in various points in the process shows where information is not flowing. In a Lean office, the desired goal is to achieve a flow of information. Work that is stalled in the email system is not flowing. The opposite of flow is a system that pushes information to the next step, hoping that the next person in line will give it high priority. Any system that pushes information from one step to the next without a clear indication of how the downstream receiver will prioritize or handle the request is a push system. Email is a push system, and as such the information is not flowing. If you have value streams that run solely via email, and most offices do, those are full of wastes and are not flowing properly. The challenge is to replace the email with a pull system.

Eliminate Waste in Your Personal Email System

Inventory:

How much inventory is in your email inbox? 100, 1,000, 2,000 pieces or more? All inventory represents work that is not moving forward. It is sitting idle. Write down the number of emails in your in basket. You may have a lot. Record your answers in Table 2.3. The goal is to zero out your inbox at least once per day

Waiting:

How long have emails been waiting in your inbox? How old are the emails in your inbox that are still waiting for your reply? Do you have unanswered or incomplete work from yesterday, 2 days ago, 1 week ago, or even a month ago? Measuring the age of the work that is incomplete is a value stream metric that quickly reveals the status of the value stream. Take a moment to write down in Table 2.3 the longest number of days an email has been waiting in your inbox.

Motion:

How many times have you opened (or will you open) emails looking for the one you need to respond to? This activity might be called "grazing" on email. People often seem to feed on their email throughout the day. People will open the email and then put it back into the inbox unopened. This is quite silly when you think about how you process physical mail that comes to your home or business. Do you read the mail and then walk it back out to the mailbox? Of course not. Yet, that is exactly how some

TABLE 2.3

Tracking Wastes in the Office Email Inbox

Waste	Waste Observed	Goal	Improvement
Inventory	*Number of emails currently in my email inbox* _____	*Goal: zero out the email inbox every day.*	
Waiting	*Oldest unanswered email in my inbox* _____	*Goal: answer every email the same day it comes in*	
Motion	*Number of times some emails have been opened and read without responding to them* _____	*Goal: open the email once and respond to it then, or log it on a list with a due date of when you will respond to it*	
Extra-processing	*The percentage of emails that have un-necessary "carbon-copied" people in the cc line* _____	*Goal: zero percent.*	

people process their email when they open it and then mark it "unread" because they don't want to deal with it at that moment.

Streamlining Your Own Email System:

Try this experiment. Create one reference folder for all of your read emails. As emails come in, determine whether they have an action item for which you are responsible. If you are responsible for the action, record it in your personal to-do list. Use a key word or the title of the email in your description of the to-do. This will allow you to easily search and find the email again. Then move the email to the reference folder. If you do not own the action for the email but want to retain the information for later reference, immediately move it to the reference folder. Move any other email to the trash. If you use this method of sorting email, you will keep your email inbox zeroed out every day, and you will have your action items clearly defined. To sustain the system, work off your action items each day and don't graze off of your incoming email. Instead, set aside multiple times throughout the day and another time at the end of the day to process email.

Replace "Push" Email Systems with a "Pull" System

In later chapters, the use of visuals to track work will be covered. The email solution involves creating visual boards between parts of the value stream that allow everyone on the team to see the status of the work. The common work is displayed so that all team members have access to it. The board should clearly show the agreed-upon due date and the person who has ownership. Colors are often used for highlighting priorities. Simple visual boards can do this easily. They are displayed in the team area. This can also be done with a simple printed list. Some teams use electronically shared lists. The only caution here is that if you use an electronically shared list, always make it a topic in the team meetings. Another best practice is to make sure that the electronic boards are displayed on a monitor in the team area. The persistent display of electronic systems helps keep the commitments in front of the team. Displayed lists are a way to create pull between team members.

Think of a pull system as a string stretched between two balls, as shown in Figure 2.1. When the second ball pulls the first one along, the string is taught. However, when the first one attempts to push the one ahead of it, the string just bunches up. The same is true between any two team members and two process steps. The downstream process or person creates the demand and signals the first process or person that the work needs to be done. This creates pull and ensures that the first process or person is working on the right thing at the right time.

These are all examples of push systems:

1. Work done by mailing the next person in the chain looking for answers
2. Work done in an order that does not reflect the customer demand (it ignores what customers want or when they want it).
3. Work done in batches based on deadlines (building up inventory) vs. completing work as it is needed by the downstream customer
4. Work done in an order that ignores the schedule by only selecting work based on first-in/first-out or by working in the order that is most convenient for the individuals

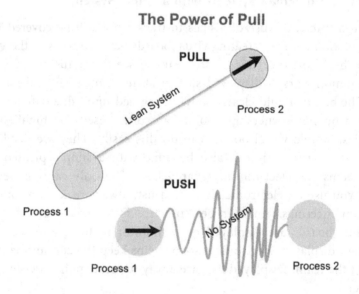

FIGURE 2.1
Lean PULL system vs. no system at all PUSH.

Most offices have any number of push systems that they struggle through every day. If push is used, then there is really no system at all. The goal of Lean is to replace the wasteful push methods with a pull system whenever and wherever possible.

These are examples of pull systems.

1. A system that uses a shared list to prioritize work from which people then work
2. Individuals in redundant different functional groups all working from the next highest priority request
3. Work done in very small batches or ideally one at a time before moving to the next item
4. All work coordinated on one schedule linked to customer demand

In Lean systems, shared lists and visual boards are used to create a common prioritized list of work from which everyone can pull the next assignment. People do not work "off the list" on their own. Daily stand-up meetings are used to keep everyone on the same list of priorities. The topics of shared lists and Lean visuals are covered in depth in Chapter 9.

How Did the Office Value Stream Get So Bad?

At this point, you might be saying to yourself, "Wait a minute, the push methods and wastes described so far fit almost anything and everything in the office." Yes, they do. That is because the office value stream was not designed to flow. Wasteful practices accumulated after years of changes and add-ons to the value stream. The lack of flow and the buildup of wastes over time are robbing the value stream of efficiency and effectiveness.

Wastes can be thought of as drags on the system. Any ship or boat develops additional drag the longer it is in the water. Barnacles and algae grow below the waterline, and they rob efficiency by making the hull less smooth. The buildup on the hull creates drag, which reduces the speed of the vessel as it flows through the water and decreases the efficiency of the engines as they work harder to maintain speed. As a result, boats and ships have to be removed from the water regularly to allow for the removal of unwanted appendages from their bottoms.

Think of removing wastes as getting rid of the unwanted barnacles from the hull of your value stream. You are trying to eliminate the drag from the value stream. In the case of wastes in the office, the goal is to eliminate the things that contribute drag. We can't afford to wait months to put our office value stream into "dry dock" to lower the fuel it needs. In the Lean office culture, wastes and drag on the system are identified and removed every day.

The buildup happens slowly over time, and it continues almost without notice. Office value streams decay slowly over time. Workers find special cases or exceptions that require extra processing and handling. Often additional work steps are added that require a lot of extra effort. Workers will add extra validation steps to trap errors and problems that occurred in the past. As the organization grows and expands, the work is divided among multiple people or even different departments. The division of labor of the process steps leads to additional waiting at the handoffs of functions and further obfuscates the value stream.

With the separation of duties and tasks across department boundaries come unwanted redundancies in the value stream. The separation also reduces the communication between workers, which further complicates the problem. Handoffs cause delays and reduce the visibility of the true customer, and the workers lose focus on the priority of the work. The workers compensate by layering on additional checks and balances in the value stream. It is not uncommon for workers to check and recheck work 4 or 5 times between process steps, which is the waste of extra-processing. Workers often perform heroics to handle emergencies in the processes to move things along. They regularly attempt to expedite work through a slow value stream. Fire fighting becomes a daily occurrence.

Over time, the decay is so severe that the original process is hardly recognizable. What once were simple and direct process steps erode into a complex and confusing mess. At this stage, the application of small incremental improvements on the process (which are call kaizens in Lean) are not enough to fix broken processes. A more radical change (or kaikaku) is required. When the process is significantly broken down, the approach of value stream re-engineering is needed. In Part II of this book, the value stream mapping approach is described in detail. The value stream mapping transformation method begins with a complete analysis of the current state. All of the wastes in the process are made visible. It is very important to make the wastes as visible as possible so that the team sees the pain they have been experiencing. They live the waste every day, and seeing it displayed allows them to tell the story. This was done in a dramatic way by the team featured in the case study at the end of this chapter. The team displayed all of the documents in the process on the wall of a large conference room. The wastes were also made visible.

What Flow Looks Like in the Office

Flow is a simple concept. The goal is to make information flow wherever it can. Never work in batches. If the work cannot flow, then use a pull system. Information should never be pushed. When work is done, it is always done to the customer demand or based on the needs of downstream processes. The opposite of flow is when information is delayed and interrupted. There is a personal element of flow. Each of us suffers from a lack of flow every day, and we have constant flow interrupters that take away time that we could spend doing the work that should be done. The office processes as a whole suffer from constant interruptions that prevent work from flowing. The primary symptom of a lack of flow is work that is done in batches. In this scenario, people don't work on the next thing that is due; they hold the work and set their own priorities. The work stops until the work is given priority by each person in the value stream reaches the top of their list. If everyone does this, then the work suffers delays at every step of the process.

There are many examples of information that is not flowing. Table 2.4 gives examples of lack of flow, with a counter example of flow and a technique for achieving it. For example, effective customer support is a frequent problem inside organizations. If a customer asks for information, but there is no clear way to get that information, he or she will be bounced from person to person trying to find the answer. We have all had this experience. Separated expertise between the call center and the people who can answer questions also interrupts customer flow. Improved flow is created when the front line of support is trained to handle the most common types of questions; then the interruptions of transferring to and waiting for another department to answer questions are avoided.

Projects depend on multiple people to complete the work; any individual can be a huge flow interrupter. If a person has critical information or expertise, and if that individual is unavailable or too busy to help the project team, the whole project is delayed.

The concept of working to customer demand and displaying those demands ensures that the work is flowing. It is always better to make the work visible instead of allowing the work to be buried.

The data catalog team at Steelcase devised a folder system to display the work as it moves through the process as shown in Figure 2.2. The team is responsible for updating over 50 product catalogs of office furniture as new products are introduced, existing products are changed, and old products are removed. Each catalog is a thick book packed with product information for the dealers who order the products. Originally, the catalogs were worked on in a giant batch with a deadline to update them every three months. This demand caused a tremendous bottleneck for the team, who struggled to meet the recurring deadline every calendar quarter. There was

TABLE 2.4

Flowing Work in the Office

Lack of Flow	Flow	Techniques
Individuals set their own priorities	Everyone on the team works based on customer demand, which is visible to all	Display the customer demand and schedule individual tasks so that the demand is met and things are not late.
Work is bundled by week, month, or quarter	Work is done per customer demand	Reduce the batch period from monthly to weekly, or weekly to daily.
Multitasking	Work on the current task until finished	Limit the work in process
A process that runs on email	No email in the process since it is a "push" system	Use a visual board to display work and use the daily stand-up meeting to set priorities and shift resources
Meetings	Minimize extra meetings	Block out no-meeting time slots for the whole team
Revisiting requirements	Fully researched requirements	Don't start work with incomplete requirements
Delayed or revisited decisions	Decisions made at the appropriate moment	Schedule the project based on decisions and use an improved decision-making process

FIGURE 2.2
An office system to create flow of catalog documents. Folders are used to show where work is currently located. A card is used to mark when work is at someone's desk and being worked on.

no flow because everything was worked on at once, and the status of the work was unknown until the very end of the 3 months. The repeating 3-month looming deadline caused a flurry of activity, and the staff put in many hours of overtime to get the work out. Staff morale was low due to the pressures on the group. The group needed a way to flow the work over the entire 3 months.

The team developed a unique visual way to display the flow of the work. Each hanging folder represented a step in the process. A schedule was devised at the beginning of the process to ensure that not everything was being worked on at once. The schedule shows the work in the backlog, which is ready to start the process.

Instead of working on the entire catalog, the team split the books into smaller units of work consisting of a few pages each. These smaller units of work are the things that move through the folders. By working on a smaller set of papers, the team can move work through the process when it is ready to be worked on. Even though all of the work on the pages happens in the computer, the work is visualized in the folders. The process was put in place a number of years ago, but it is still used today. It has been perfected, but the basic concept remains the same.

The pages are placed in the folder signaling that work is ready to start the next step. The team reviews the folders every morning at their stand-up meeting and checks on the board throughout the day. When an individual is ready for the next piece of work, he or she walks up to the visual wall and "pulls" the next set of pages. The team creates an "out-card" to show who has the work. The out-card signals that the pages are being worked on, and it tells who is working on them. Since the out-card has a time in and time out for each step, it records the amount of time that work is being done. The board shows the status of work throughout the day in real time. At the stand-up meeting, the team members give updates on the status of the work. Any flow interrupters are discussed at this time. They become clearly visible because the work is not moving across the wall. The team members also discuss what they have finished and when they will be ready to start on the next set of pages.

The work flows through the process steps each day. At the end of the value stream, the team assembles the work into the catalog books to complete the process. The whole process flows now, and the large batches of the past have been removed from the process. The work is more manageable, and it is fun for the team to see the status of work on any given day. The leader of the team is much more aware of the status of the work. On any time of the day, the visual wall tells both the team and the leader the status of the work. They know what yet has to be worked on. They know what work is in process. They know what work is completed.

The catalog team increased the work through the system and now meets deadlines without the pressures of having the deadlines run the process. The team also took in work that was previously sent outside the company and realized over $2 million in savings. They also reduced the catalog cycle from 3 months to 2 months. Now, they regularly process catalogs on a 2-month cycle. Some electronically produced catalogs are produced weekly. The reduction in the overall cycle time means that the downstream customers get updates on products and learn of new products being offered in a timely way.

Why All Office Value Streams Have 50% Waste before Improvements

Wastes are all around us every day and in every value stream inside organizations. In fact, the wastes in your value streams might be as high as 90%. When you first look at your value streams, you will find that at least 50% of the work is wasteful and in need of improvement. As your mind starts to think in terms of wastes and information pushed through the process steps, you will start to see wastes everywhere.

The waste of waiting for information and decisions is prevalent throughout the office. This causes flow interrupters to the work. Work starts and stops many times before being completed. Every work stoppage puts a delay in the information value stream. If the value stream is full of interrupters, the work sits idle. In the office, this is so prevalent because the work is not visible. It is hidden inside people's email, in paper systems, or in a workflow in a computer system. Every time there is a handoff between process steps, there is a potential delay. At the point of handoff, the next process step is often not ready to accept the work. This creates an interruption in the system. When interruptions occur, the ratio of time spent doing actual heads-down work versus the actual time spent working on things quickly builds up. It is not uncommon to see a ratio of 10 to one between the amount of time work sits idle and someone actually performs a task. The number of handoffs and idle, non-value-added time versus active, value-added work time are two measures of process wastes.

Another in-process metric is the amount of rework in the process. Rework is anything that is done internally to improve the quality of the output. Office processes often experience 20 to 50% internal rework at many steps during the process. Office workers often perform heroics to make sure the customer is satisfied. The end quality is achieved, but only by correcting the work along the way. Instead of the end quality, a more complete measure of the poor quality in the process is a measure of the completeness and accuracy of the information as it moves through the process. The measure of how smoothly a process is flowing can be gained by looking at the quality at each step. Poor incoming quality at any step will cause interruption and a loop back to a previous step to correct the information. Information completeness and accuracy of incoming quality ranges are needed for

TABLE 2.5

Typical Value Stream Process Metrics

Waste Measure	Description	Typical Office Numbers
Number of handoffs	The number of times information is passed between individuals in the value stream	10 to 20
Rework	The percent of work that has to be sent back to an earlier step for corrections or for missed information	20 to 50%
Completeness and accuracy	A measure of the incoming quality of each step in the value stream; it is measured between the steps in the process. The value stream will never be better than the weakest link.	40 to 60%
Overall cycle time	A measure of the total time needed to complete the entire office value stream from beginning to end	Days to months

different steps in the processes. Any of these quality errors left uncorrected could potentially leak through to the end customer, but office workers typically perform heroics to correct these things and they never reach the end customer.

Table 2.5 shows the typical metrics to describe the effectiveness of a value stream. Handoffs and idle time both contribute to the lack of flow of information through the processes. The time from the beginning to the end of the process is rarely known, let alone measured, in an office process. Yet, it is the key measure that the customer at the end of the process experiences. The overall time (or total cycle-time) through the process measures the duration of the process. It is a measure with direct effect on the customer.

The customers receive the output at the end of the value stream. They are "looking from the outside in." They actually experience the effectiveness and efficiency of the work being completed. They experience the delays.

CASE STUDY – PRODUCT DATA TEAM

At Steelcase Inc., the Grand Rapids based furniture manufacturer, Lean was first applied to the office in 2003 in the IT department, which created the data to support new products. The current state was complex, and the team took a rather creative approach to showing the process and noting the wastes in the process. In the workshop, the team was asked to bring into the room all of the documents representing a data build for a new product and to place them on a time line. Every document represented a significant task in the process, as shown in Figure 2.3. When work was handed off from one person to another, a paper hand was placed on the wall. At any place at which work stopped, a stop sign was placed on the wall. Other process problems were noted on 3 x 5 blue cards pinned to the wall.

The project wall demonstrates in a very visual way all of the complexities and wastes in the process. Instead of treating it as an embarrassment, or hiding the problems, the team actually left the wall up for a number of weeks to show what they had to deal with on a daily basis. They started calling it their "Wall of Shame." The process problems were significant and summarized by the team in this way:

- It took 9 months to develop data from beginning to end.
- 50% of the effort was due to rework.

FIGURE 2.3
Office wastes displayed and made visible.

- Multiple redundancies were built in to track errors.
- There was significant wait time.
- The process contained more than 60 handoffs.
- It literally took longer to build the data than it took to physically tool the product.

The "Wall of Shame" was a creative way to visually see the wastes and point to the problems in the process. It was a way to make the wastes visible for everyone on the team and to everyone outside the team. Other teams regularly had meetings in the room and were able to see all of the wastes. It was shared with the management team and even with the company executives. Making the wastes transparent, and not hiding them, was a new behavior in the Lean culture. Wastes and problems are exposed and worked on, not buried. By exposing the wastes, the team could then tackle the job of removing them and improving the process.

A future state value stream map guided the improvements. The process wall showing the wastes informed a number of kaizens (or improvement activities). The team focused more on process improvements than on automation or enhancements to the IT systems. This ensured that the process was fixed first; otherwise, the danger is to automate a flawed process.

The management team reorganized the groups into teams arranged by the type of work they were supporting. This concept was similar to the Lean work cells used in the plant to create flow. Each team now contained members who were originally from different departments. The team members brought to the table all of the skills needed to complete the tasks of building the data. The co-location of the team dramatically reduced the number of handoffs and removed interruptions to the flow of the work. The team created a visual project board to track the progress of each project. They changed their behavior and thought of all of the projects as one batch of projects with a common due date, and now they look at the flow of each project from start to finish. On a visual control board (shown in Figure 2.4), when an individual project was ready to start, they marked it with a ready indicator. If there was a flow interrupter for a project, it was marked on the board with a red flag. The status of all projects was reviewed in a daily, 15-minute, stand-up meeting.

The results were dramatic.

FIGURE 2.4
Visual board in the office to track projects.

- The cycle time was reduced by 50% from 9 months to 4.5 months.
- Rework across was reduced from 50% to less than 10%.
- The productivity of the teams improved by 30%.

The product data teams had the right combination of cultural factors to make Lean a success. They had a strong desire to change. After showing their "Wall of Shame," the case for change was apparent and always in front of them. The team had a willingness to learn how Lean could help their project. They brought in Lean coaching from the manufacturing side of the business to apply Lean concepts. The leadership, from the vice-president and director to the managers, was engaged; it championed and believed that the Lean methodology would improve the process. The leadership was process oriented and believed that if the process changed, the work environment and morale would be improved as well. The teams also showed that the goals could be set high and that they could be met or even exceeded.

The team started out with some rather unique goals to create a culture of problem solvers. Everyone was to feel part of the solution and part of a well operating team. The team described the new desired environment:

- Everyone feels part of a well operating team
- A team is full of great utility players who are cross-trained
- People feel they can share issues openly
- Workers are part of implementing the solutions

- There is a willingness to look upstream and downstream from the present responsibility to identify and fix process problems

The team gained the help of some Lean experts from the manufacturing side of the corporation.

The initial successful experiments in the product data area energized the Lean implementation in the company, and the concept of rolling Lean out across the office side of the organization seemed plausible and feasible. The concept of a steering committee took root on the executive team, and an external consulting group was brought in to teach Lean methodology in a larger way in the company. The Lean journey had begun and would be sustained over the next dozen years. The early success in a key area was the motivation to expand Lean across the office. Other teams working on other types of data creation applied the same techniques and reduced their cycle times even further. For example, the service parts team, which applied similar methods to their data creation, improved their cycle time from 6 weeks to less than 5 days, and they more than doubled their productivity. They also cut their errors in half. These initial successes in the early days of the program sparked interest across the organization. The organization launched dozens and dozens of improvement projects. Over the next several years, the result was over 150 Lean improvement projects across the company.

SUMMARY

The One Main Thing – Make the wastes visible and work to eliminate them by replacing "push" systems with "pull" systems.

STUDY QUESTIONS

1. What are examples of wastes as they translate to the office value stream?
2. What is an earmark of a Lean culture that is eliminating wastes?
3. What makes email a push system, and why should it be eliminated from the office value stream?

4. What does flow look like in the office value stream?
5. Why are typical office value streams filled with between 50% and 90% of wastes?
6. What are some typical value stream metrics that are used to track the wastes (or inefficiencies in the process)?

3

Organizing for Lean Success

BEGIN WITH THE END IN MIND

One of the primary goals of the Lean transformation inside an organization is to look at the value streams that span the departments and functions. Every organization has several important business value streams that repeat in the customer-facing process over and over again. Lean in the office involves searching out problems in a value stream across the departments in order to make the needed changes and improvements. I once heard Jim Womack speak at a conference, and he gave the simplest and most elegant definition of Lean that I have ever heard. He defined Lean thinking as, *"Thinking horizontally, across the verticals."* That is to say, Lean thinkers spend their time thinking about and improving the value streams that cross the various organization boundaries and departments.

Office Lean examines how information and data flow through the value streams across the departments in the organization as shown in Figure 3.1. Typical high-level office value stream examples include the following:

- From sales to order (from initial customer contact to order)
- From order to cash (from taking the order through payment)
- From order to shipped product or service provided
- From customer support request to issue resolved
- From product concept to product design delivered to production

In Lean, the first principle is to consider the value produced for the end customer. The value for any office value stream is defined from the point of view of the end customer. The goal of a Lean office culture is

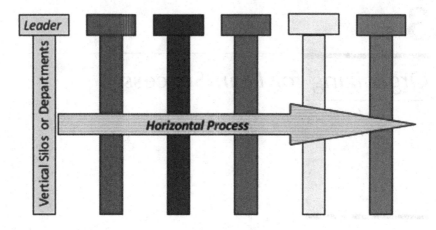

FIGURE 3.1
Value streams across organizational boundaries (from David Mann, creating a Lean culture).

straightforward: The Lean office optimizes the value that the customer receives from the value stream, while removing the wastes or problems in delivery the product or service. Any and all wastes that prevent the customer from being served are targeted for removal in the office Lean value stream. The fact that value is always defined from the point of view of the end customer, as shown in Figure 3.2, is a central theme in all of Lean. For the office, the end customer resides outside the organization. He or she is at the end of the value stream chain. Lean in the office seeks to optimize the end customer experience by removing the wastes, reworks, delays, and errors.

Since the value stream crosses multiple organizational silos, the organization of the Lean initiative needs to account for the difficulties of working across multiple silo-ed individuals or departments. However, the conventional organization is structured into functional areas. The functional view is always the strongest and is a more dominant voice inside the organization. The goal of the Lean initiative is to make the value stream view more dominant. With the process steps clearly visible, the disconnects and wastes can be analyzed and minimized. The goal, however, is in direct conflict with the power and strength of the functional structure that is dominant in most organizations.

The value stream does not appear on the org charts in most organizations. Instead, we find separation of duties by skills reporting to

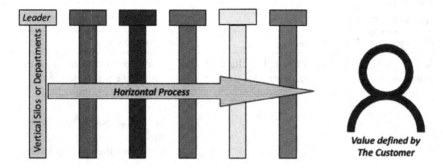

FIGURE 3.2
Value in Lean is defined by the end customer.

a functional leader. The functional leader holds positional power and budget dollars and controls resource assignments. The value stream has no positional power, no budget assigned, and no dedicated resources. The functions are measured in various ways, but the value stream is rarely measured. The most striking difference is that the functions focus on internal order, but the value stream focus is on the customer. The customer experiences all of the good process steps and any wastes that pass through the value stream.

OVERVIEW OF THE VALUE STREAM MAPPING TRANSFORMATION

The Lean office endeavor is not a project or a program. The ultimate goal is to develop a culture in which the entire organization is continually working on the cross-functional value stream. The Lean office program follows a series of principles that are embedded into the organization (see Table 3.1). Central to all of these is the concept of employee involvement in the transformation. Leaders and staff are equally involved in the transformation. The leaders set the expectations and goals and are involved in improvements as much as the staff. In the office, small inter-department wastes are removed by the staff and the managers. The manager and staff are involved with other departments to regularly look at cross-functional value stream projects. To drive the cultural transformation, both the

TABLE 3.1

Lean Office Principles

Principle	What it Means	Keys to Success
Seek customer value	Customer receives the value desired from your value streams without any unnecessary trouble	• Always describe value from the customer's perspective, either the external or internal customer. • Remove all non-value-added steps • Streamline the rest of the steps
Continuously improve	Lean is a journey that is never done. Never be satisfied with your current condition.	• Leaders constantly ask the organization to make the next improvement and are actively involved in making improvements at their own level in the organization. • Staff never stops working on the improvements. • Work on the little improvements as well as the larger projects. • Over time, transform into a culture of continuous improvement.
Leadership is involved	Lean activities are organized and coordinated across the organization. Leaders set the vision and standards for each area.	• Leaders practice Lean themselves. • Leaders allocate time for improvement across the organization at all levels. • They teach the importance of continuous improvements.
Work on the value stream	Recognize the work of the office as value streams, and work to make them more efficient.	• Work on critical value streams. • Break value streams down into areas that can be worked on. • Look for wastes and opportunities to improve the flow.
Employee involvement	All individuals in the organization are involved in the improvement effort.	• Staff is involved in defining the future state and owning the improvements. • Everyone works on value stream improvements. • Finding improvements becomes a daily part of everyone's job.

large value stream mapping exercises and micro improvements need to be tackled.

In most organizations, the value streams at a high level are too large to be tackled at once. They need to be understood as sets or sequences of value streams that make up the whole. Each one will be broken down into various sub-value streams with short implementation targets of 90 days or less. Smaller pieces of the overall value stream are the focus of the exercises outlined in Section II of the book, which covers the workshop methodology. The basic improvement methodology is executed over and over.

Document the current state

- Review Lean concepts.
- Draw the current state value stream map.
- Identify the wastes in the current state.

Design the future state

- Apply the Lean principles that will improve the value stream.
- Draw the desired future state value stream map.
- Present to and reach agreement with the affected leaders.

Create the kaizen improvement plan

- Create the improvement plan for the kaizens.
- Present to and reach agreement with the affected leaders.

ORGANIZING FOR LEAN

The senior leadership needs to provide the focus on the most troublesome value stream problems. The leaders will need to build the case for change by pointing to the value streams that need to be improved and setting aggressive goals for making the improvements. The leaders need to set the stage for working on the office value streams. They will build the case for change and the need for a Lean office program. Too often people are comfortable with the status quo; often, they are not aware of the wastes that exist in the overall value stream. Remember the focus is not on sub-optimizing one part but on making the whole value stream flow seamlessly. This value stream focus requires leadership to shine a spotlight on which value streams need some work and then point the improvement efforts in that direction.

The teams doing the improvement work will face challenges and roadblocks working across the organization that lack a value stream focus. The senior leadership helps the teams remove any barriers and roadblocks as they attempt to make the changes. The importance of change management by leaders cannot be under estimated. The resistance to change in most organizations is strong, even if the change is for the better. Leaders need to reassure staff members that they are not fighting a losing battle. The leaders need to constantly encourage. The leaders also need to emphasize the shift to a culture in which change will be steady and part of how the organization operates on a daily and weekly basis going forward.

I often hear questions about the need for senior leadership involvement in the transformation. People wonder if the initiative can start at the bottom and grow organically, but the level of transformation required to create a culture of continuous improvement takes more than a bottoms-up organic growth model. Senior leaders play a critical role in aligning the organization around the transformation. The leaders need to teach Lean principles, ask their teams to work on improvements, and practice Lean for themselves at the leadership level. When we cover the various types of visual improvement boards in Section III of the book, there will be examples of leader improvement boards that need to exist in parallel with team improvement boards. The leaders play a very important and active role in the Lean transformation.

CHARACTERISTICS OF A LEAN LEADER

The Lean leader is the spokesperson and champion of the Lean way of thinking, demonstrating by actions and daily activities a commitment to the Lean program. The idea that waste elimination is everyone's problem and that all value streams can be improved is a key element of their message. The leader not only gives the message; at best Lean leaders become the message. The concept that improvement is always needed and possible is an important message. This message was demonstrated to me in a rather dramatic way early in my own Lean journey. I was called in along with some other Lean champions to help with manufacturing problems for an existing chair manufacturing line. This line was well established and producing several hundred chairs per day. The plant manager was clearly a Lean thinker. After giving us a tour of the existing layout and talking to us about some of the existing problems, he gave a challenge. He said that many people thought of the line as already fully "Lean" and optimized; however, he was convinced that there were significant improvements to be made in the layout and flow of the line. He told us that while it was running well, there were still too many opportunities for errors and too many chairs ending up in the "hospital" at the end of the line. The challenge he outlined was to reduce the footprint by 50%, improve the flow path, and install significant error proofing techniques. Oh, and by the way, the goal was to do all of that in 90 days or less. This was a significant challenge, and it demonstrated his philosophy that significant continuous improvement was always possible. The leader was a true Lean thinker and doer.

Shingo said that "The best approach is to dig out and eliminate problems when they are assumed not to exist" *(https://Leansixsigmabel gium.com/quotes/shigeo-shingo-quotes/, et.al.).* The Lean leader is a problem seeker. The Lean thinking leader creates an environment in which people can continue to learn and grow. The Lean leader demonstrates the following personal behaviors:

- Becomes a student of Lean
- Teaches people how to problem solve and apply Lean principles
- Encourages all team members to take risks and use mistakes as learning opportunities
- Discusses lessons learned from difficult situations
- Recognizes individual and team efforts in problem solving
- Holds himself or herself accountable for problem solving everyday
- Walks the value streams personally to observe improvements and look for additional opportunities for improvements.

The Lean leader also is responsible to set up the program initially to ensure the effort launches successfully. The program needs a fair amount of care and feeding in the early months. The leader

- Appoints Lean champions to help roll-out the Lean initiative
- Sets up the structure for the Lean program
- Sets up a regular cadence of checking in with the Lean champion team on the progress of projects

The senior leaders can do this effectively by appointing a community of leaders who share the responsibility of directing the efforts of the Lean champions. They can provide guidance on which areas of the organization have the most nagging problems. The group can also monitor the progress of the various projects in flight. The leaders also gain firsthand knowledge of the improvements by looking at the contributions to the value stream at with the team. The leadership team will also ask key direct reports to sponsor Lean projects and sit in on workshops to act as leader participants.

The involvement of the direct reports on the Lean projects is a key ingredient in the Lean workshop model. It might even be called a secret sauce. The leaders who own the various parts of the value stream need to be supportive of the team documenting the current state, uncovering the wastes, and then finding a new improved future state to correct things. The workshop model brings these direct leaders into the workshop as the future state is being designed.

With a few key activities, the senior leaders can leverage a few hours of effort every month to support the entire Lean program.

CHARACTERISTICS OF A LEAN CHAMPION AND FACILITATOR

The Lean champion and facilitator of value stream mapping sessions in the office has some unique skills as described in Table 3.2. Since the Lean champion will be working across the various departmental barriers inside the organization, the champion needs to develop skills to work between departments, in the white spaces across the corporation. The champion needs to have skills to facilitate groups and lead people in the right direction, but the champion will not come in and make all the changes for the team. The team has to adopt the Lean philosophy and make the changes for itself, and the champion has to help the team change its focus and direction.

TABLE 3.2

Skills of a Lean Champion

1. A passion for and intense commitment to Lean
2. A change agent with impatience for the status-quo
3. Ability to teach one on one or in small groups
4. Ability to think on one's feet
5. Comfortable in front of leaders and executives
6. Tolerance for ambiguity and uncertainty
7. Ability to apply Lean concepts to any team

The role of the Lean champion requires a different set of skills than the organization typically seeks out to fill office positions.

Lean Champions Have a Passion for Lean

The Lean champion needs to have a passion for Lean and an intense commitment to it. I suppose the first quality is obvious. The candidates for the Lean champion role should believe that Lean will make a difference inside the organization. They may or may not already be experts in the topic of Lean; however, they should be completely devoted to learning everything that they can about Lean. The Lean champions should quickly apply Lean concepts to their own environments both in the office and at home.

Lean champions should never be satisfied with the status quo. They will have a passion for making the value stream better. Yet, their impatience with the status quo will be tempered by the ability to be patient with individuals making bona fide efforts toward change. They will not sit back and wait for the system to improve; instead, they will be on the forefront helping to make it better. Lean champions seek change, and they have an intense commitment to Lean as an improvement approach. They deeply believe in the ability of individuals to contribute to improvement in the value stream, regardless of their position or status.

Lean Champions Are Change Agents

The Lean champion might be known by another name, the change agent.

A successful change agent recognizes the opportunity for change and seeks to make it happen. The change agent has a clear vision of how

Lean will help and is patient yet persistent to make change happen. He or she asks the tough questions such as why things are the way they are today and why they can change. The change agent is very knowledge-able about change and seeks to make change happen. Relying on other experts to augment their knowledge, change agents constantly rea about Lean and see ways to apply Lean to new problems.

Lean Champions Are Teachers

The need for the Lean champion to teach perhaps is obvious. He or she will be constantly teaching and instructing and helping the people think in Lean ways. The settings for teaching Lean might be classrooms or the organization. But the Lean champions will teach in many situations where problems and issues need to have Lean principles applied. The Lean champion will need to teach in a variety of situations: one on one, in small groups, in large groups from prepared material, from impro-vised material, and from live observation used to illustrate principles or applications. One common situation into which Lean champions are frequently thrown in as facilitators of workshops. The Lean champion is a patient teacher, helping learners apply Lean principles to their setting. They are patient yet firm. They also often teach using the Socratic method. That is to say, they use leading questions to help learners work through the problems on their own. They do not give the answer, even if they know what it is. They give the learners/students time to think for themselves, knowing that the lesson will stick when it is internalized.

Lean Champions Can Think on Their Feet

My own memory of learning Lean under David Mann, my Lean sensei, includes many times when Dr. Mann would ask me to observe a situation with problems and wastes and then ask me "What do you see?" On one occasion, we were in a manufacturing plant looking at an assembly line, and he asked, "What wastes do you see?" It was up to me to think through the list of wastes and find examples. Then he would ask for each waste, "What would you do to remove the wastes?" As a newbie at Lean and someone who was very respectful of Dr. Mann, that was difficult. I really had to think on my feet. He was patient and waited to give any answers while I thought through the situation. He would ask other leading questions, "If you see this waste, what other ways have you seen that would tell you what to do in this situation?" A Lean student must have conceptual speed and the ability to think on his or her feet, as well as to apply lessons from one set of circumstances to new situations and to explain the lesson clearly and understandably to people who are trying to apply Lean concepts for the first time to their own situations.

Lean Champions Are Comfortable in Front of Leaders

The champions' skills need to include the ability to form a personal, tutor-student relationship with front-line staff and the teams doing Lean, but also the managers, leaders, and executives in the organization. The champion is the coach to the whole organization and has a responsibility to help connect the roles across the value stream. When working across the value stream, Lean champions find themselves in front of various department heads who often have competing goals and challenges. The Lean champion helps leaders see the waste in the value stream. They help to shine a spotlight on the wastes between the steps in the value stream, so that they are exposed. With the proper attention placed on them, the wastes have to be dealt with. The Lean champion coaches the leaders to look at the problems, without calling attention to the people in the process. The Lean champion helps the leaders understand that their job is to create a safe zone or a spot immune from finger pointing. They focus only on the problems and seek to find ways to solve them. The Lean champion is always coaching the leadership on how to encourage and empower the team to make their own improvements. This is a very different management posture than the traditional command-and-control management system in which "I'm the boss. You're the employee. I call the shots, and you will do what I say." In Lean, the employees are given the authority to change the system, and they are encouraged to do so. The Lean champion coaches the leaders at this level. It is a difficult assignment, and the Lean champion must feel comfortable teaching and coaching leaders that might be 1, 2, or more level higher in the organization. The Lean champions facilitate discussions across the levels during workshops and in 1-on-1 meetings. The ability to facilitate discussions across the levels is an important skill.

Lean Champions Have a Tolerance for Ambiguity and Uncertainty

The Lean champions have to work in situations where the wastes are obvious, but the solutions to removing the wastes and making the value stream more efficient may not be clear. The challenge is to know as much about the steps in the value stream as possible before changing it. If a value stream is particularly complex, it might take days to understand and uncover what is really going on inside the work and the systems used by the workers. Initially, the Lean champion will not know as much about the work as the people in the value stream, but they are a quick study. While the champion may not ever know everything that goes on inside the value stream, he or she gains enough understanding to facilitate the group. This requires the ability to live with a degree of uncertainty or ambiguity about the value stream. The champion will learn enough about the value stream to recognize where the wastes are and where the process steps should be improved. Intuitively, he or she will know when to be able to confidently coach the team and point to some solution options. The ability to coach while not seeing every little detail requires a tolerance for ambiguity, to operate in an environment where not every detail of the value stream is known, but enough is known to make appropriate suggestions. Lean champions will need to be able to work out solutions with the team by helping the team see the wastes in the value stream and to know which Lean tools could be applied to remove the wastes. The goal is to get the buy-in of the team and the leaders. The champion coaches the team on how to apply Lean concepts but allows the team members to submit their ideas on how to get there. This is an area of low certainty for the champion surrounding how solutions or improvements will be put in place. Yet, even with uncertainty in the team or with incomplete knowledge of the value stream, the Lean champion can guide the team to the correct solution.

Lean Champions Are Able to Transfer Lean Concepts to Any Situation

Lean champions are students of Lean and can apply Lean concepts to any situation in which wastes exist, and wastes exist everywhere. However, those wastes need to be exposed and carefully handled. The champion uses his or her ability to see the wastes and expose them to the team. However, exposing wastes can be difficult and might uncover interpersonal raw spots. The champion is very sensitive to people's feelings and has a high degree of what is call emotional intelligence. The champion is a good listener. This means there is an ability to understand others' points of view on a particular subject as well as their emotional points of view and probable worldview and to relate to people across a wide range on these attributes. This almost empathic ability with people helps the champion expose problems and suggest solutions. The champion often runs into corporate politics and baggage from the past and has to be able to carefully acknowledge the baggage and carefully unpack it without upsetting individuals. The goal is to leave the unwanted process steps outside of the new solution going forward.

The Lean champion has a unique set of skills, is selected based on the ability to apply Lean to any situation, and will have demonstrated the ability to apply it to his or her personal world at work or home. The champion is also selected based on software skills and the ability to teach, coach, and work with teams. In Lean, the goal is not to make the improvements for the teams, but rather to help the team make the improvements.

CASE STUDY – STEELCASE LEAN ACTION COMMITTEE

Late in the fall of 2003, Steelcase Inc. executives decided to expand the Lean manufacturing initiative into the office world. Lean had been highly successful in manufacturing, and many within the organization credited Lean for major improvements and efficiency gained that helped the company weather the economic downturns in 2002 and 2003. The senior leadership team created the Lean Action Committee (LAC), which consisted of 4 executives: the president, the vice president of human resources, the VP from manufacturing (who had largely been responsible for the improvements and gains there), and the CFO. The committee of four met monthly to help direct the new Lean initiative, check on progress, and help remove barriers and roadblocks as needed.

The committee appointed a director of Lean in the office, which was David Mann, and a team of 5 internal Lean consultants. These internal Lean champions were responsible for learning how to transfer Lean concepts from manufacturing and apply them to the office value streams. The internal Lean consultants were handpicked from within the company. They had already shown a passion for Lean and an aptitude to learn everything about applying Lean in the office. They were demonstrated change agents and had earned influence and respect across the company.

The executive LAC met monthly to direct the Lean consultants on what areas of the organization should be targeted for Lean improvements. At the request of the company, the newly assigned Lean champions created highly valued maps of the high-level value streams inside the corporation. After analyzing the systems and work, and documenting the high-level wastes, the order to cash stream was selected as the value stream that needed the most focus, so the team was directed to start in this area.

The LAC asked the process leaders to support Lean transformations in their areas, and the Lean consulting team went to work mapping the sub-value streams in detail. People were trained and workshops where held. Whenever possible, the training was done as close as possible to the workshop. The just-in-time model of training ensured that the concepts were fresh.

The outputs of the workshops were A3 improvement plans. The LAC asked for these report-outs on the progress each month; however, they did this is a very creative way. One month the LAC would meet formally to review project plans. Project plans were presented on a one-page (A3 size, or 11 x 17 inch). On the alternate month, the executives would tour the team areas and look at the value stream maps and improvement activities A3 in the area where the work actually took place. The leaders went to the actual teams doing the improvements. This Lean office executive Gemba walk brought them to the floor where the improvement work was getting done, and they talked to the people doing the actual work and making the changes and improvements to the value stream. The alternating focus on strategy and projects the 1st month, and detailed project review on the next month, was a pattern that the LAC used throughout the first years of the roll-out of the Lean initiative.

This was a level of leader involvement was not common in the office. The manufacturing plants had witness the behavior from the VP in manufacturing who attended many kaizen events. Now his peers in the office were being asked to practice the same behaviors in the office. This was new and uncomfortable for some, and to help with the new behavior the executives were paired with the Lean champions who took them on the process improvement reviews with the team. The Lean champions coached them through the Gemba walks. The Lean champions gave them an overview of where the team's work fit into the larger, overall value stream, and then they helped by giving them the questions that they should ask. The questions help the execs connect the improvements with the business results. This gave the executives the confidence when entering new areas of the company. This level of involvement was important for the teams to see and experience, and the executives came away with firsthand knowledge on what changes were being made by the teams. As the teams ran into roadblocks, the executives were able to take away specific things to talk about and actions that they would own.

SUMMARY

The One Main Thing – Lean leaders learn Lean and practice Lean for themselves, so they can demonstrate the Lean behaviors for the organization.

STUDY QUESTIONS

1. Where is the customer of a Lean value stream found? Can you site some examples?
2. What is the leader's role in tackling value stream improvements?
3. What are some of the activities of a Lean leader?
4. What are the skillsets of a Lean champion?
5. What is the role of the Lean champion in working on office value streams?

SUMMARY

STUDY QUESTIONS

4

Getting Started

The Lean Office Initiative

STEPS FOR SETTING UP THE OFFICE LEAN INITIATIVE

In the last chapter, the importance of naming an executive steering committee was described. The role of this committee includes creating the framework that will be necessary to ensure the success of the Lean program inside of the organization. In the early days of the Lean initiative, there are many things to do: name a person who will be in charge of the Lean office, name the team, train leaders and the team, create the idea system for employee involvement, pick the first projects, etc. However, a most critical element of launching a Lean program involves giving the right message to the organization on the philosophy and purpose of Lean.

The initial message is critical, and the message needs to come from the leaders in the organization. Furthermore, the same message should be repeated by all leadership across the organization. The right messaging helps to reinforce the Lean initiative so that it will become part of the culture. It sets the stage for what is coming. It should also dispel fears that people may already have but may not necessarily be willing to verbalize. Positive messaging involves emphasizing how the Lean initiative will help the organization in several ways.

- Lean is first and foremost an improvement system. It involves working on problems that have plagued the organization for many years.
- Lean is common sense. Lean draws on the existing knowledge of the staff closest to the work. The staff comprises the people best suited to work on improvements because they understand the methods and standards of the work. Lean respects the people in

the process and their skills and knowledge of the work, and it trusts their ability to improve the systems.

- The Lean improvement cycle is never done. The idea of ongoing continuous improvement will become part of fabric of the organization.
- With Lean, everyone will be involved in improvement. The expectation is that leaders and workers alike will be involved in making improvements to the systems. Lean looks for the involvement of everyone in the organization.
- Lean is not just for the experts. Anyone can learn the Lean wastes and the principles to remove the wastes by applying systematic improvements.
- Lean is a way to improve the entire enterprise. The organization will ask everyone to think about the value across the whole value stream.
- Lean can be simple and fun. Improvement kaizens will become a way of life.

Just as important as the positive messages, the potential negative messages need to be anticipated and countered from the start. Many people will have heard of Lean or experienced it at another organization. Since there might be preconceived negative notions concerning what Lean is all about, several myths have to be dispelled right from the start. People may have heard that Lean is about cost cutting, which it is not. They may worry that people will lose their jobs as a result of Lean, which is not the intent of Lean at all. They may have heard that "Lean is mean," and it is not. It is better to verbalize the fears underlying Lean implementation.

- Lean is not a cost-cutting program. Lean is an improvement methodology that will bring increasing value and efficiency to the organization.
- No one should lose employment because of Lean. Lean is about making improvements that will help the organization become more fit, efficient, and competitive.
- Lean is not a program or project; it is a way of life. Lean is a lively verb. Lean involves doing things to constantly improve the work and systems.

People will often voice that they are already too busy and over-burdened and they do not have time for making improvements. This is a common complaint, and it is true of course in many organizations. People are often so busy struggling with broken value streams that they can't imagine carving out any time for making improvements in order to improve their situations. This is a proverbial "Catch-22." People don't have time to make improvements, and because they never work on improvements, they are forever too busy to create a better process. The Lean program has to carve out daily time for people to make improvements. My experience and coaching have proven that even small investments of 5 to 10% of a work week (2 to 4 hours per week) are enough for teams to implement significant positive change in their work places. The Lean office workshop methodology in Section II of this book shows how to effectively leverage people's limited amount of time.

Some companies have adopted Lean during periods of economic downturn or downsizing. Tying Lean to reductions in the workforce has the potential to give Lean a negative message. People might believe that LEAN stands for "Less Employees Are Needed." This negative thinking needs to be intercepted. Lean is first and foremost about improving the value stream and then growing the organization, and no one loses employment because of it. If the organization has to down size to survive, this should be done outside of the Lean initiative. In other words, downsize first, then put the Lean program in place. There are also examples of companies that have stepped up their improvement efforts during slower economic conditions. They have used the time to make significant improvements and focus on growth. The message of respect for people should be stated clearly and often. People come first in Lean. This message helps to build the Lean culture.

Besides setting up the Lean program, the best methods for building the Lean culture occur when the leaders practice the Lean principles for themselves. They cannot merely give lip service and talk about the importance of Lean, they must practice improvement on a daily basis. In the latter chapters, the topic of leadership involvement and a parallel system of leader improvements will be described. If the leadership is unwilling or untrained to make improvements on problems at that level, then the changes in the Lean systems will not be sustained.

THE IDEAL INTERNAL CONSULTING TEAM

In the initial weeks and months of the Lean initiative, the organization will rely on external experts to bring education and Lean techniques to the office. This will help the organization launch the program, but there must be internal resources available to learn from the external experts and then to extend the practices throughout the organization. This is why the internal Lean team is central to building the culture. The team will take the learning and knowledge and apply it across the organization. Whether the Lean team consists of part-time or full-time resources, the members should be passionate about Lean and seek to practically apply it. Ideally, they will be assigned to the Lean initiative for several years to give continuity to the program.

Organizationally, the Lean team should report high enough in the organization to give it the authority to tackle tough problems. The director or leader of the internal Lean team should report directly to the executive steering team appointed to oversee the Lean efforts. When the Lean team reports to this level, the message will be sent out that this is an important and significant effort. This is especially needed in the early months and years of the Lean transformation.

Over time, as the improvement techniques and tools are practiced throughout the organization, the need for this reporting relationship diminishes. However, until the Lean culture takes hold, the Lean program will need emphasis within the organization and a degree of positional power to push it forward. The case study at the end of the chapter from Calvin College gives an excellent example of an organization that established the executive sponsorship at the right level in the organization. The Lean program reported directly to the vice president of administration, and it had the support of the cabinet of the college. The Lean team reported directly to the vice president and reported regularly to a steering committee on the progress of its efforts.

The Lean team should have enough depth and bench strength to tackle the value stream improvement projects that are targeted by the leadership. The ideal size of the internal team is 4 to 6 full-time members for a mid-size organization. Larger organizations will need to scale up the team to handle multiple sites or divisions. If there are multiple sites and divisions, then each one will have a small team devoted to leading the effort in that part of the organization. In this case, the dispersed teams will report to a central Lean organization, as shown in Figure 4.1

The internal consulting team comprises the keepers of the workshop standards, and they will become the experts in the methodology.

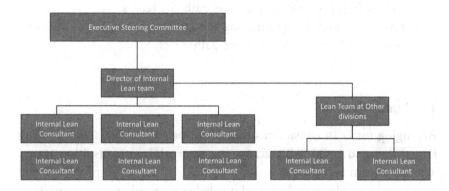

FIGURE 4.1
The Lean team structure.

Initially, the members of the internal consulting team are the only ones providing expertise and knowledge of the methods to transform the culture and improve the value streams.

The duties of the internal consultants involve setting up best practices and demonstrating them. The key activities include:

- Creating an education program
- Delivering the training with the leadership of the organization. The foundation of the Lean system is that members of the leadership are the leaders and the coaches.
- Setting up the workshop methodology to ensure successful workshops
- Working with the business leaders to identify areas for value stream workshops
- Preparing leaders for their role in value stream workshops
- Facilitating value stream workshops
- Defining the action plan with the project manager for value stream mapping projects and converting it to a single A3-style project plan
- Following up with improvement kaizens that are defined in the workshops
- Helping teams define the visual control system that will allow the work in the value stream to be visible
- Coaching teams on the methods of making continuous improvements and helping them set up their own "improvement board"

- Celebrating progress and success with the teams
- Promoting and communicating the Lean wins across the corporation in writing and at employee gatherings

The Buddy System

Arranging for Lean consultants to work in pairs provides a way to share knowledge and build skills across the internal Lean consulting teams. The Lean team is often called upon to tackle some tough problems, and having two people to gather the knowledge on a value stream and then co-facilitate the Lean workshop is highly effective. One person can be interviewing and making observations while the other is taking notes. Having two people looking at a value stream issues and problems provides additional insights. When the internal Lean consultants facilitate workshops, there is a power in having two people facilitate the group. One person will be leading the discussion, questioning, and listening carefully, while the Lean buddy is capturing points on flip charts and drawing the value stream map, and there is a lot to capture during the work. The goal in a value stream mapping workshop is to make the work, with all its good and bad details, visible. The workshop room walls are typically full of documents, post-it notes, value stream map drawings, action steps, ideas, parking lot items, etc. There are many details to capture; a Lean facilitation buddy is an important asset in documenting all of the details that emerge during the workshop.

Facilitation of a value stream mapping workshop is difficult and tiring work. Figure 4.2 shows my Lean buddy facilitating a workshop while I take a break and take a picture of the group. Facilitating a day-long workshop is like running a marathon. My wife knows that at the end of workshop days, I am often exhausted. I go home in the evening, sit in my recliner, and often fall asleep. A 2- or 3-day workshop has a cumulative tiring effect, and I am even more tired at the end of each day. Having a partner during the long workshop days makes the workshop less tiring and produces a better facilitation result.

On more than one occasion, I have needed a mental break from facilitating a workshop, and I have relied on my Lean buddy to relieve me for a few minutes. In one situation, a few participants in the group I was facilitating with my buddy were becoming impassioned and resisting the forward progress of the rest of the team. At one point, the

FIGURE 4.2
My Lean buddy Jon is co-leading a value stream mapping workshop with me (the author is taking the picture).

participants were extremely confrontational. Often this is a good time to take a break and come back a few minutes later when everyone is fresh, but in this case we had already taken a break and a few of the team members were still driving the team in the wrong direction. I don't remember exactly what I said, but the essence of my comments was that the group in the room had worn me down. I told them that I was frustrated with the team and needed a break. I gave the whiteboard marker to my Lean buddy, Steve, and I walked out of the room. Normally, I am a very patient person, but my patience was stretched to its limit. My buddy was able to use the opportunity to discuss with the group the impasse that had been reached, and the team was able to find a way forward. Steve gave me a needed break, and he used the opportunity to help the group come to a resolution.

My Lean buddy was there to allow me to remove myself from the workshop before I blew up and said something I would have regretted. This tag team effort is important; on many occasions, my buddy and I spent breaks, lunch, and time at the end of the day discussing ideas for moving the team to a solution. Sometimes the way forward is not entirely clear, and there are team dynamics to navigate. Having a buddy there to discuss ideas and potential solutions provides a way forward. We review and unpack the workshop and discuss strategies for the next day. We talk about the application of potential Lean principles and strategies for how to move the team forward.

USE OF EXTERNAL CONSULTANTS

In the early months of the program, the internal consulting team will need the support of experts. An external consultant with experience in applying Lean in the office, not just in manufacturing, is a must. The nuances of applying Lean in the office warrant someone with experience in translating Lean concepts to the office area. The external consultant will provide education for the team. Ideally, the consultant will create a train-the-trainer program and teach the internal Lean team to teach and facilitate across the organization in the future.

ROLES AND RESPONSIBILITIES ACROSS THE ORGANIZATION

The internal Lean consultants will do the following:

- Create an education program for the staff and leadership
- Set up the workshop methodology and standard work
- Set standards for visual boards
- Set up a structure, cadence, and responsibility for reporting on progress
- Set up a daily improvement program
- Free up time for the Lean team to devote to training and projects
- Celebrate successes and regularly communicate on projects

The internal consulting team will also help individual areas set up their own continuous improvement idea systems (as described in Chapter 10 in the section on Tier I – Team Based Improvement Systems). The idea system is a critical piece of building a Lean culture and should be put in place as early as possible.

The Role of the Project Managers

The internal consulting team will soon have a capacity problem if it also serves as the project manager, following up with every improvement kaizen identified in a workshop or on an improvement board. If it is held responsible for ensuring that all kaizens are completed, then the team's capacity is greatly diminished, and it will have less time for working with other areas of the organization.

The project management duty is one that must be assigned for each Lean project, and it will help make the implementation successful. The internal Lean consultants will need to identify and appoint a project manager within the organization to take responsibility for improvement activities. The project manager will follow the project from the beginning with pre-scoping and scoping activities, all the way through the end of the workshop. (Pre-scoping and scoping are meetings with the leaders responsible for the workshop; they are held to define the purpose and objectives of the workshop. Pre-scoping and scoping are described fully at the beginning of Chapter 5). Table 4.1 outlines the duties of the project manager at a high-level. Ideally, that person should be someone from the area of the value stream who is willing and motivated to improve work methods and to drive out waste.

SELECTING THE FIRST PROJECTS

The first projects will be at the direction of the Lean steering committee. These should be medium-sized projects, with clear objectives and opportunities for improvement. The goal is to obtain some early wins. The success of the first areas is important for showing credibility of the Lean techniques. After the initial projects, word will quickly get out to the organization, and you will want the message to be positive. There should be clear communication of Lean improvements. As

TABLE 4.1

Duties of the Kaizen Project Manager

Prior to the workshop:
- Attend pre-scoping and scoping meetings (as described in the beginning of Chapter 5). Complete the scoping documents. End out invitations to the workshop participants and workshop leadership panel. Attend the homework sessions.

At the workshop:
- Attend all sessions. Some project managers will take an active role in facilitating discussion and capturing the results.

After the workshop:
- Schedule follow-up kaizen meetings. Schedule weekly updates with the kaizen owners. Draft and update the kaizen project plans with the kaizen owners. Create a visual wall for the display of the improvements and the kaizens. Collaborate with the internal Lean consultants when kaizen teams need help. Schedule the 30-, 60-, and 90-day follow-up sessions with the leadership. Update measures and benefits.

---

demand grows, the internal Lean consulting team will have plenty of value stream work to tackle. Then, the internal Lean consulting team will want to create a pull system of its own. This will involve a backlog of projects kept on a list. The projects will be selected by a number of criteria that measure the impact and value to the customer of the value stream.

- Projects should focus on the complete end-to-end value stream.
- Value streams should include steps that start and/or end outside the four walls of the business, ensuring that the customer of the value stream has a direct voice. Either the sales force or the customers will then be directly represented on the workshop team. This gives an "outside in" view of the value stream from the perspective of the true customers. If it is not possible to have a customer in the workshop, a member can take the role of the voice of the customer.
- The best value stream mapping sessions are achieved when all of the players in the value stream are brought into the room together. This provides the greatest opportunity for learning.
- The people who do the work are the best candidates for the workshop. The goal of the Lean value stream mapping exercises is to uncover the real, true work that goes on inside the value stream. The people closest to the work understand it the best and

should draw the value stream map and discuss improvements. The managers and leaders are not as close to the work methods or the systems. Don't assume that they know the work as well as the people in the value stream; likewise, don't assume that they are best suited to own the action items to improve the value stream.

- The whole value stream map is drawn from beginning to end. The goal is to be as complete as possible and show the entirety of the value stream.

Managing Multiple Projects

Once the internal Lean team is fully staffed and up to speed, it will be able to handle multiple improvement value stream mapping projects while teaching and coaching teams on methods of improvement. Each Lean team pair should be able to handle 4 to 6 projects simultaneously. Projects are typically tracked on their own visual board as shown in Figure 4.3. Since individual projects are typically in different stages in their life cycle, the Lean team can maintain a pace that allows it to work on multiple projects at once. This means that on any given date, some projects will be in the scoping phase, others in the workshop phase, and some in implementation.

Projects are tracked by their progress though pre-scoping, scoping, workshop, implementation, and the leader meetings at 30, 60, and 90 days. An analog visual board such as the one in Figure 4.4 is an excellent tool for tracking the multiple projects in flight at any given time.

A simple visual board can be used to track completed Lean projects and capture and record the benefits achieved. In Figure 4.4, each project appears on a one-page visual sheet. Those on the left will be reported on in the next team meeting of the office Lean consulting team. The right side represents recently completed projects, which have completed a report-out. It is recommended that the benefits of completed projects of the Lean practice be captured and recorded in a database or spreadsheet for tracking.

Measuring the Benefits

The Lean program will create significant benefits for the organization, and senior leaders will ask about the progress. In the first phase of the Lean rollout, measures should be on two criteria:

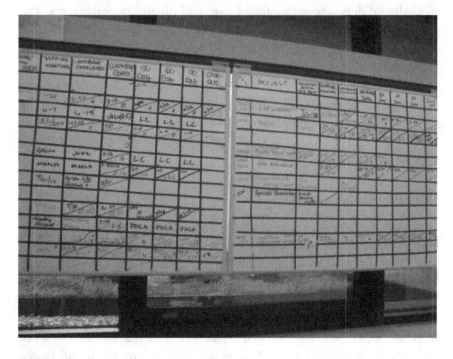

FIGURE 4.3
The internal Lean consulting team project board. This is tracking the status of multiple Lean projects per person.

1. Involvement in the program
2. Improvement of the value stream

Some leading indicators of these are the following:

1. The number of departments involved in some form of Lean improvement activity
2. The number of kaizens or improvements made in each area
3. The before and after improvement metrics for the value stream

Improvement metrics track improvements in processing time, cycle time, and quality before and after Lean workshops or kaizen events. Since most value streams are full of wastes, the goals for improvement can be set quite high. A goal of 50% is not unrealistic.

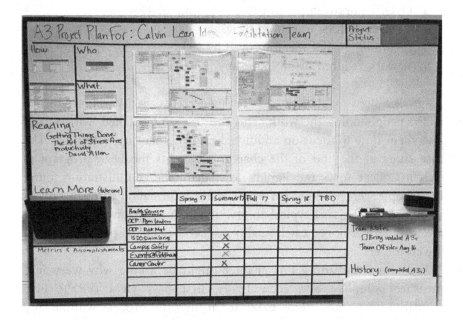

FIGURE 4.4

The college Lean team visual project wall.

You will notice that all of the metrics in Table 4.2 target an improvement of 50%. We simply call this the 50% rule: As a result of value stream improvement projects, expect a 50% reduction in processing time, overall cycle time, quality problems and rework. Through my experience and tracking, actual results across all of the Lean projects show alignment with the 50% rule. The results were reported for each project and averaged across all of the projects in the organization.

TABLE 4.2

Value Stream Metric Goals after a Lean Workshop

Process Measure	Definition	Target
Processing time	• The amount of time spent doing the work in the value stream; often called "heads down time"	50% reduction
Total cycle time	• The total elapsed time through the value stream	50% reduction
Improvement in quality	• A measure of the incoming completeness and accuracy for the steps in the value stream	50% increase
Rework	• Any tasks repeated that require people to return work and correct errors	50% reduction

- Overall improvement in processing time of 43%
- Total cycle time improved by 45%
- Incoming quality was improved by 45%
- Rework reduced by 50% or more

As process steps are eliminated or re-engineered, capacity will be returned to the people doing the work. This can free up burdened workers and give them time to focus on additional improvement opportunities. The case study at the end of the chapter highlights the Lean program at Calvin College in Grand Rapids, Michigan. The administration found that people were working heroics to move information through broken value streams. This is a typical observation in many organizations: People are working heroics to catch quality issues so as not to pass them on to the customers.

Lean experts reading this chapter might be asking why we would measure complete and accurate vs. first pass yield (FPY)? FPY describes how many items make it through the process without any issues and problems. It is used in manufacturing as a measure of quality of the products moving through the manufacturing value stream. Products without any defects at the end of the value stream increase the FPY percentage. However, in an office value stream, the work moving through the value stream is often fixed along the way. Because nearly all of the problems are corrected (not all of course), the FPY percentage is artificially high. The issue goes back to heroics. In the office, knowledgeable workers recognize quality problems when work reaches their desk. At this point, they will often quickly correct them so as not to move problems to the next person. We are thankful that conscientious workers are catching issues before they reach the customer. However, because of this common behavior, a good measure of the quality within a value stream is the quality of the work coming into each process step. This measure is the percentage of the work that is "complete and accurate." It can be thought of as the ability to perform the work step without returning the work because it is incomplete or contains errors. In Lean manufacturing, there is a measurement of the FPY, the amount of a product that makes it through the process without any quality defects.

The common Lean metric of FPY through the value stream is not measured in the office because of the reasons stated above. Instead, the measure of incoming quality highlights the misses before they are corrected. This helps filter out the problems in the handoffs between the work steps.

Much of the savings from Lean improvements is what financial analysts call "soft savings" because they don't reach the bottom line on first analysis. For example, if 15% of a person's work is eliminated, not enough time is saved to reassign the work. However, the elimination of tasks does raise the capacity of the person by 15%. This might relieve an over-burdened worker. Cumulatively, across the team in the organization, all of the improvements lead to an increased capacity of the team to do more work. It is difficult to measure the impact to the organization of the incremental savings of individuals. Even if only a small percentage of time is saved by an individual, the savings across the entire team over time make a significant impact. There is more capacity to do work and an opportunity to rebalance the workload.

While metrics can be tracked to show improvement, the number one goal in a Lean cultural transformation is to change behaviors and practices in the organization. The culture change observed in a Lean organization shows transition away from a top-down improvement system to a team-based approach in which everyone in the organization is focused on waste removal and improvement.

CASE STUDY – A COLLEGE TACKLES A LARGE VALUE STREAM TRANSFORMATION

Calvin College, a liberal arts college located in Grand Rapids, Michigan, was founded in 1876 by the Christian Reformed Church. The college sits on a beautiful campus and has an enrollment close to 4,000 students. Calvin is ranked number one in the Midwest compared to other regional colleges. In 2014, the college embarked on a Lean journey.

The college was introduced to Lean by Russ Bloem, the VP of enrollment. He was encouraged by Calvin's distinguished alumni Dale and Mary Andringa. Dale was on the Calvin Board at the time, and his wife Mary, as CEO of the Vermeer Corporation, had led a significant transformation based on Lean principles in the operations of the industrial equipment company she led. They were eager to see Calvin reap the benefits of Lean. Bloem was also on the board of the Fuller Theological Seminary in California where he learned firsthand how Lean could be used to transform value streams in higher education. Both connections piqued the interest of Bloem, who wondered if Calvin College could have a Lean program.

With seed money from a donor, the college explored options and began researching Lean. One of the first activities was to gather a group of leaders from across the college for an investigative trip to California. In January of 2014, Bloem organized a trip to Fuller with Todd Hubers the vice president of people, strategy, and technology. They brought along a group of leaders from the college including the CIO, the directors of health services and the physical plant, the dean of students, a representative from the Provost's office, and the director of employee relations who would soon be named the coordinator of Lean at the college. While on the benchmarking trip, they talked to the Lean team at Fuller and witnessed a Lean workshop firsthand. The group of 8 came back energized and ready to start a Lean journey at Calvin College.

Upon returning from Fuller, Hubers was appointed to lead the program at Calvin, and the college ran some early Lean experiments. In one experiment, they invited Fuller to come to Calvin to run a Lean workshop on campus. The workshop gave them some initial, firsthand experience on the benefits of value stream mapping workshops. During this time, they also collaborated with the Reformed Church offices in Grand Rapids. The Reformed Church in America is a close sister denomination to the college. So, you could say they crossed the denominational aisle to learn from another organization that had already deeply embraced Lean to improve its administrative value streams. Benchmarking other Lean initiatives is an important step in launching a Lean program.

The Lean initiative lost a little steam after the initial activities, and it needed an active steering committee to move it ahead. Hubers formed the steering team and then formed an internal Lean consulting team. This gave the college the organizational structure it needed to run and sustain a successful Lean program. Deirdre Honner was appointed as the Lean coordinator, and 8 people were selected from across the departments to form the internal Lean consulting team. The group of 8 was assigned part time to the Lean program in addition to their other responsibilities. Members were promised to have some time freed up for Lean, and, as an outcome of their Lean work, would enjoy the benefits of applying Lean to their own departments. The bandwidth of the team varied by individual and fluctuated across the college's annual calendar, but with all 8 committed to the Lean efforts, they had enough bench strength to significantly push the Lean initiative forward.

Immediately after the internal Lean team was formed, I engaged with the team. Additional training and benchmarking took place. The internal consulting team visited local Lean implementations in Grand Rapids at the Steelcase corporate offices, the Fire Department of Grand Rapids, and AMWAY. It also attended various meetings and events with the Michigan Lean Consortium. The team attended the Lean training at Steelcase and saw firsthand the implementation of a Lean management system in the office. The Calvin team rallied around Lean concepts and called itself the Lean Idea and Facilitation Team or LIFT. Most often, around the campus, this name was shorted to the Calvin College Lean Team.

The energetic team quickly embraced Lean. The initial value stream mapping workshops were guided by the author based on the model practiced at Steelcase. LIFT learned the workshop model for some meaty value stream problems in the areas of human resources, financial aid, provost faculty appointments, and new user access to information technology. From these early successful applications of Lean, LIFT quickly started to facilitate workshops on its own in numerous areas across the college. These included Lean improvements made in accounts payable and receivable, campus safety, in the career center, and with disability coordinators.

LIFT had some notable successes: By repeatedly applying the workshop model, it made significant gains in removing wastes and improving the value stream. In one example, it removed all of the wastes in manual paperwork completed by the disability coordinator. By streamlining the work, all paper was eliminated, and the work was moved into the college computing system. As a result, by the time a new person was brought on to do the work, the job had changed so much that the person could also be assigned other tasks. In another situation, improvements allowed an employee, in the onboarding department, to reduce her workload. Marcie was a 30-hour employee who was working 45 hours, 15 hours every weekend. After fixing and reducing the work steps and improving the information flow coming to her, she could go home with her work completed after her allotted

30-hour workweek. Lean is a success when the employee goes home and the work is done.

LIFT made its work visible to the college. It set up a visual project board in a hallway and held weekly stand-up meetings at the board. The board was about 40 feet from the president's and provost's offices in a high-traffic area. People took notice and frequently asked about the Lean activities.

In addition to the numerous workshops the team completed, other college departments had caught the "Lean bug" and were starting to implement Lean on their own. Idea boards started popping up in departments around the campus and started to fuel change as the staff identified wastes and generated ideas for value stream improvements. Idea boards in the departments of health services, music, college advancement, the physical plant, and information technology were driving continuous improvements and additional benefits for the college.

In one example of employee-initiated improvements, a campus building services lead, Sandy, suggested using fishing line to create accurate spacing of the rows of chairs in the fieldhouse. The initial prototype pole with fishing line is shown in Figure 4.5. The fieldhouse is used for indoor sports events (like basketball games) and large student events (like graduation). The fishing line idea spawned the idea of using a string on two poles. Sandy reported that the first prototype worked but had issues. Unrolling the string was difficult, and it was easy to get knots. The sticks were not sized properly to the aisle space, and extra boards were taped to the ends to get the right aisle measurement. Rewinding the strings on the boards was also frustrating.

After using the initial prototype, an improvement was made. A set of hinged boards able to be unfolded to 9 feet (the correct aisle spacing), was created in the college workshop. One board is placed at the front and the other at the back of the auditorium, and a chalk line (with chalk markings at the proper intervals) is stretched between the ends of the boards. The new invention, as shown in Figure 4.6, saved 15 hours per month, and it allowed the set-up crew to create perfect rows of seating in the college fieldhouse.

The culture was changing in other positive ways. Deirdre, the Lean coordinator, noted that improvements were no longer just from the "top down." With Lean, people were able to talk about how they were going to make their own jobs better. She observed, "The Lean team were the facilitators who were looking for ways to improve processes and help the people. We listened to the struggles of the staff." Lean enabled

FIGURE 4.5
The initial college fieldhouse row spacing prototype device.

a renewed level of trust and communication; teams could discuss real value stream problems. Lean also gave the team new tools to improve work steps for themselves. In one instance, the Lean team received a request to run a student employment workshop for on-campus jobs. However, after an initial discussion, the department stated that it had enough knowledge from other Lean workshops and felt able to facilitate.

FIGURE 4.6
The college employee improvement to fieldhouse set-up. This idea saved time in setting up perfectly aligned rows of seating for large campus events.

In another example, the Calvin Information Technology (CIT) department used Lean methodology to complete an entire reorganization.

Matt Hoekzema, from the college's facilities and physical plant department, was one of the original 8 internal Lean team members. He led the financial aid workshop that dramatically re-engineered the financial aid value stream. This was made possible when the government allowed the use of prior year tax returns in 2016 for granting financial aid. The financial aid kaizens were placed on a visual wall where the team held weekly update meetings. Matt states, "The goal is to always go back to the visual, one-page project plan. It is important to keep bringing the team back to the problem statement and the improvement plan." He notes that when the value stream is made visual the team can rally around improving it and moving to an improved future state. Matt notes that Lean requires ongoing focus. "Even today – it is too easy to say I don't have the time to make the time for the changes.

The reality is that you have to make the time for improvement to get the rewards."

The Calvin Lean team's work was noticed across the college. In 2017 just 3 years into their journey, the Lean team was nominated by peers around the campus for the president's Team Spirit Award. This high-profile award is designed to recognize staff and teams who go beyond expectations in contributing to the college's mission and who exemplify outstanding achievement and/or service. There were numerous other nominees for the award, but there was strong support for the Lean team.

One person commented, "I think that the LEAN team should receive this award. They have done a great job helping many departments across campus improve and rethink their work. This cross functional team exhibits true teamwork, collaboration, and continuous improvement." Ultimately, based on the strong support and recognition across the college, the cabinet and president voted to give the Team Spirit Award to the Calvin College Lean Team.

The college is still maintaining their Lean culture momentum. In 2017, Deirdre turned the reins of Calvin's Lean program over to Lucas Moore in the information technology office. The internal Lean consultants are still leading workshops. Additionally, the college is offering a Lean course to all departments that has been well attended. Most importantly, individuals continue implementing Lean improvements on their own.

SUMMARY

The One Main Thing – the Lean team plays a central role in advancing the Lean culture inside the organization.

STUDY QUESTIONS

1. What are the right messages to deliver about a Lean cultural transformation?
2. What messages should you avoid delivering, and counteract against?
3. How are people and their jobs viewed in a Lean transformation?

4. What are the practices of Lean leaders?
5. What is the role of the internal Lean consulting team?
6. What is the Lean buddy system, and why is it important?
7. What is the role of external Lean consultants vs. the role of people inside the organization?
8. What are the roles and duties of the project managers in the value stream transformation? Why is this role critical to the capacity of the organization to make improvements?
9. What are the typical measures of the benefits of the value stream improvement activities?

Section II

Office Value Stream Methodology

5

Pre-Project Contracting and Scoping

Office work can be improved by focusing on the end-to-end value streams in the organization. The purpose of the value stream focus is to uncover the wastes throughout and between the steps of the value stream. This end-to-end focus follows the business across the functional silos and departmental boundaries, with the ultimate goal of satisfying the needs of the primary end customer. The workshop model, shown in Figure 5.1, works through a series of steps to set up the workshop and ensure its success.

CONTRACTING FOR THE SUCCESS OF THE VALUE STREAM MAPPING WORKSHOP

In the first step of contracting, the leaders must come together and agree to the project. The challenge of focusing on the end-to-end value stream is that the value stream steps cross many functional silos, with separate functional leaders who are responsible for only their piece of the whole. Because of the separation of work by function, the first step in scoping is to align the leaders and have them come together to reach agreement on the breadth of the value stream and to have them give some direction on what could be improved. Since the leaders in the scoping meeting most likely report to different department heads within the organization, they are the first to put on their Lean googles and look across the functional boundaries in the organization in a spirit of solidarity to cooperate and fix a broken value stream.

Lean Workshop Model

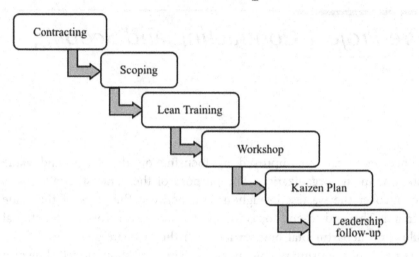

FIGURE 5.1
Value stream mapping steps.

PRE-SCOPING AND PLAYERS IN THE VALUE STREAM TRANSFORMATION PROCESS

The internal Office Lean Team or the Lean expert who has been charged with working on the value stream improvement project will need to set up an informal "contract" with the functional leaders responsible for the various parts of the value stream. In this stage, the leaders have to understand Lean at a high level, and they have to agree that a workshop method is the best way to tackle the change. The leaders must agree to

- focus on a specific value stream (or part of the value stream),
- look at wastes without pointing fingers across the functional aisle,
- assign workshop participants from their area,
- reserve some capacity of the workshop participants to improve the value stream over the next 90 days,
- be involved in the workshop,
- stay involved in the improvement efforts and support the plan for improvement,

- be available to remove barriers and roadblocks when the team gets stuck,
- understand that the work that occurs in the value stream (and the ugliness of the wastes) will be made visible, which might be uncomfortable for them, and
- be prepared that if the project goes red, it will be shown, and that red should not be hidden, because it provides a chance for course correction.

The leaders and stakeholders need to be brought together in a leadership panel. We will see that the leadership panel, made up of the key stakeholders, stays with the value stream transformation efforts. They play an important part in setting up the effort and participate in the workshop itself; they stay connected to the team as it starts the hard work of changing the work methods in the value stream.

Not all change requires a full workshop, and some do not need a workshop at all. During the discussion about the Lean workshop, it is not uncommon for the leaders to conclude that the issues or problems can be solved by making other changes to the work steps, staffing, or even adjusting policy. If the wastes can be eliminated without a workshop, then it doesn't make sense to do a workshop. I was involved in a project for which the workshop was not needed. As the value stream was described, it became evident that there were too many approvals built into the process and that they were causing delays. The head of the organization reviewed all decisions for the spending of funds. During the scoping session, it became evident that a particular policy was causing waiting and rework in the value stream. The excessive approvals could easily be eliminated with a change in the policy of who made the decision to spend money. The change needed was a policy correction that gave more authority for the managers to approve spending within their budget and up to a certain dollar value. The organization just needed to change the policy of what the managers needed to approve. Once this was done, then the approvals were streamlined.

The Roles of Leaders and Stakeholders

Several roles need to be specifically assigned for the duration of the value stream mapping project. These roles are explicitly named and are listed on the scoping document for the workshop.

The Business Owner/Project Sponsor

The business owner is the sponsor of the project. As previously mentioned, the leaders of the various functions across the value stream have to be brought together for the scoping session and then stay together for the duration of the Lean workshop. The business owner has the responsibility of organizing the value stream project and pulling the leaders together.

The business owner will:

- participate in the scoping meeting,
- set the objectives and goals of the workshop,
- align the leaders who are responsible for the parts of the value stream, and
- ensure that the right resources are on the project.

The Stakeholders

The stakeholders are the leaders of the functions in the day-to-day running of the value stream. They are the leaders with the responsibility for the workshop. The stakeholder

- participates in the scoping session,
- helps the business owner set the objectives and goals,
- assigns the workshop participants to the project, including a project manager for the effort,
- attends the workshop to review the future state map and kaizen plans,
- helps the team remove any roadblocks during the kaizen implementations, and
- Holds project reviews with the team at 30-, 60-, and 90-day intervals to look at the progress of the kaizens.

The Value Stream Manager

In most organizations, there is no one person responsible for the overall value stream. The value streams are split across multiple leaders in the organization. Still, one leader should be appointed to have overall responsibility for the value stream. The person who is closest to the customers of the value stream is the logical choice. Their primary responsibility is to represent the customer of the value stream during the workshop. They will also own the value stream after the workshop is done. The workshop may have completed successfully, but the improvements on the value stream have only started.

The Office Lean Facilitator

The office Lean expert is a person with Lean knowledge and background who is named to lead the team and facilitate a workshop. The facilitators come from the team of internal Lean consultants. They must be trained in facilitation techniques, and they have to be able to apply Lean principles to improve projects. Their role is to

- facilitate the scoping session,
- understand the value stream in enough depth to see the wastes and opportunities for Lean improvements,
- train the workshop participants on seeing and removing wastes,
- facilitate the value stream mapping workshop,
- teach Lean concepts to the workshop participants,
- fully document the workshop outputs (current state map, future state map, and kaizen plans),
- work with the project manager who owns the improvement kaizens coming out of the workshop
- follow-up with the stakeholders as needed when road blocks occur,
- attend the weekly kaizen review meetings, and
- attend the 30-, 60-, and 90-day update meetings with the stakeholders.

The Project Manager

The desired outcome of the workshop is the identification of the kaizens (kai translates as change and Zen as good. So, kaizen means "change for the good" in Japanese). Each kaizen to improve the work steps will be documented with a detailed A3 project plan. The kaizen plans will be documented as an outcome of the workshop. However, they will also need some oversight to ensure that they are accomplished. The workshop facilitator (or internal Lean consultant) can provide this project management oversight. However, if the organization hopes to leverage the internal Lean consultants on multiple projects simultaneously, it is better to assign the ownership of implementing the kaizens to a project manager. The project manager will

- attend the workshop,
- own the A3 project plans that result from the workshop,
- hold a weekly kaizen update with the kaizen owners,
- own individual A3 project plans, and
- hold the 30-, 60-, and 90-day review meetings with the stakeholders.

The Ideal Workshop Team

The participants in the Lean workshop should include the people closest to the actual work. They know the work steps the best, and they know where the wastes are in and between the steps. A good workshop guideline is to exclude managers and leaders. This allows the employees who are closest to the work (and the problems) to speak freely. Having a dominant leader in the room can inhibit people from sharing. The leader may also try to direct the future state discussions with a personal view of the solution. In Lean, the goal is to have the people who are closest to the problem solve it. So, during scoping session with the leaders, it should be made clear that the leaders will not be in the workshop itself, during the mapping of the current state, or during the creation of a future state map. Instead, they will be brought into the workshop when the future state is ready to be reviewed and again when the kaizen plans are ready to be discussed and committed to. Some leaders will push back and want to be in the workshop. Unless the leader is directly involved in the day-to-day work in the value stream, this should be discouraged for a couple of reasons. First, the desire is to have the people closest to the work draw the map to show what actually happens in the value stream. They know the work the best, and they know the spots where the work processing is broken. Second, the staff might be intimidated by having the leader in the room, and they may not want to reveal all of the problems. They don't want to look bad in front of their leader, and they will be quiet. In Lean, the goal is to expose problems. Shigeo Shingo said, "Lean thinking leaders look for problems where none are thought to exist." The leaders responsible for part of the value stream have to encourage the participants to expose the problems across the entire value stream. Not every problem will be fixed as a result of a single value stream mapping session, but problems should be made visible so those that are critical for a smooth flow of work are addressed with kaizen improvements.

SCOPING GOALS, OBJECTIVES, AND MEASURES

The scoping session kicks off the workshop process. It is a meeting with the business sponsor, the stakeholders, and the Lean facilitator. It sets the objectives and measures and defines what is in and out of scope for the workshop. The outputs of the scoping session are

- the goals and objectives for the workshop,
- assignment of the leadership team from the stakeholders,
- Identification of the project manager,
- Identification of the workshop participants,
- workshop logistics, and
- the scoping document.

The scoping document is called a SIPOC, which standards for Suppliers, Inputs, Process, Outputs, and Customers. It is a one-page document, see Figure 5.2, on an A3 (11" x 17") sized sheet of paper. The goals and objectives are listed at the top of the SIPOC, and the measures are on the bottom. It is a high-level overview of the process steps and sets up the workshop. The SIPOC becomes a one-page guide for the workshop team, and it is used to kick-off the workshop. It gives the team a great starting place for the discussion and mapping of the value stream. Often during the workshop, the facilitator will point the team back to the goals and objectives. These ground the team and return the focus to the purpose. There are many "bunny trails" of discussion in any value stream discussion, and the goals and objectives are used to return the team to the primary purpose of the workshop.

The goals and objectives for the workshop should be clearly spelled out during the scoping session. The goals typically describe the problems to correct across the value stream. These are high-level statements that make the case for the improvements. A typical problem statement at the value stream level outlines the impact to the business. For example, a typical goal (or problem statement) for a value stream might be the following:

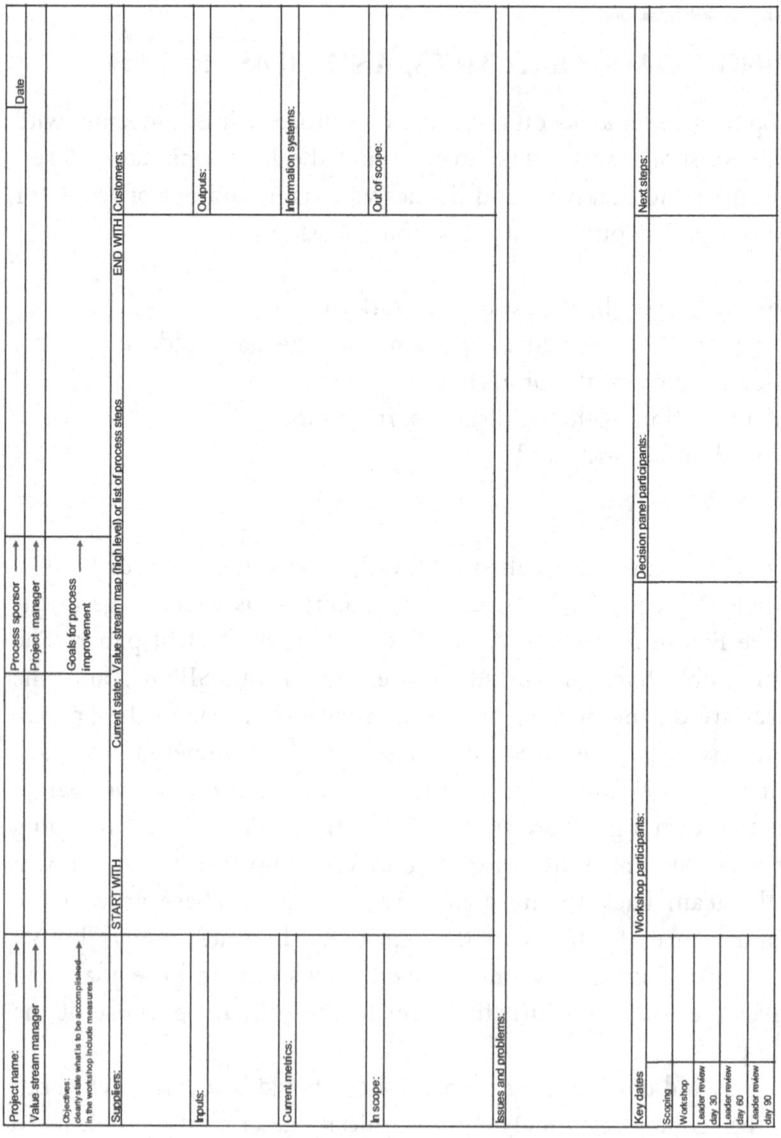

| Project name: | | Process sponsor | | Date |
| Value stream manager | | Project manager | | |

Objectives: clearly state what is to be accomplished in the workshop. Include measures.

Goals for process improvement

	START WITH	Current state: Value stream map (high level) or list of process steps	END WITH	Customers:
Suppliers:				
Inputs:				Outputs:
Current metrics:				Information systems:
In scope:				Out of scope:

Issues and problems:

Workshop participants:

Decision panel participants:

Next steps:

Key dates	
Scoping	
Workshop	
Leader review day 30	
Leader review day 60	
Leader review day 90	

FIGURE 5.2
The SIPOC.

The value stream involves multiple handoffs and calls for multiple redundant approvals. This results in delay, customer complaints about our responsiveness, and vulnerability to competitors with faster processing.

This can be broken down into bullet points on the SIPOC form:

- Avoid multiple handoffs
- Reduce approvals
- Reduce customer complaints and delays in our services.

The 3 goals above would be listed as the goals on the SIPOC.

The objectives break this down to the what should be accomplished in the workshop itself. Typical objectives include:

- Reduce rework and handoffs in the value stream by 50%.
- Reduce the number of required approvals from 7 to 1.
- Reduce the value stream cycle time from 72 to 24 hours.

The 3 objectives above would be listed in the section of objectives on the SIPOC.

The objectives are written in a way that they can be measured. Each one should have a specific, measurable, aspect that emphasizes the current condition and where the team should be heading. The objectives and measures should be aspirational. Many times, when they are first presented to the team, the team will believe them to be very difficult to achieve. But, they need to be challenging enough to impress on the team that the value stream must be transformed. In Chapter 2, we noted that all value streams easily contain 50% waste. Each measure should attempt an improvement of at least 50%.

HOMEWORK AND WORKSHOP PREPARATION

After the scoping session, the Lean facilitator starts to prepare for the workshop. Since the workshop participants have already been identified, the Lean facilitator uses the time between the scoping session and the workshop to understand the work steps in more detail by talking with the people closest to the work. Spending time with the participants also gives the facilitator some credibility with the people who will be participating in the workshop.

The participants will realize that someone really does care about the work and the difficulties and challenges that have to be overcome every day.

The facilitator walks through the value stream person by person on an office "Gemba walk" (Gemba is a Japanese word roughly translated as the place of the actual work). However, since the office work is not visible, as it is in manufacturing, and the work is mostly buried in the computer systems or email streams, the facilitator interviews the participants who will be in the workshop to understand their work. Starting somewhere at the headwaters of the value stream, the facilitator follows the information flow downstream through all of the work steps. Typical questions asked by the facilitator are:

How do you know when to start?
What information do you get from others?
What is (are) your work step(s)?
What IT systems do you use?
What screens in the IT system do use? Can you show me?
What is the output of your step(s)?
Who next in the value stream gets that information?
What problems do you experience?

While asking the questions, the facilitator is taking notes and sketching what the value stream does, who is involved, where the handoffs occur, and how the work flows (or doesn't flow). Some of the processing wastes are discovered at this time. Many more will come out during the workshop session itself.

Besides getting an initial picture of the wastes, the facilitator gains an understanding of the value stream and meets the people who will be in the workshop. The facilitator should draw an initial value stream current state map. I regularly do this when facilitating workshops. It may never be shown to the team, but it is a starting point, and it gives me an initial understanding of the flow of work.

CASE STUDY – AREA EMPLOYMENT GROUP USES LEAN TO HELP JOB SEEKERS

West MichiganWorks!, a division of ACSET (Area Community Service Employment and Training) Council, is a government-sponsored organization for the development of jobs in a 5-county area. They partner with employers, economic developers, and community organizations to create a qualified workforce that meets the region's current and future talent needs and fuels the shared economic future of West Michigan. After learning of the benefits of Lean and looking at work from a value stream perspective, the agency found a good fit for the application for a value stream mapping project. The organization's internal method of matching job seekers with employers was in need of improvement.

The leadership team, including the chief operating officer, Angie Barksdale; the regional director of business solutions, Deb Lyzenga; and the regional service director, Brittany Lenhertz, identified the need and kicked off the workshop. The 5 counties had been recently merged into 1 organization. The leadership trio had the assignment of standardizing the work of connecting job seekers to local employers across 5 county offices. Each office had its own version of the work of matching job seekers with local businesses looking for talent. The leaders knew the work methods were different at each one of the 5 county offices, and they lacked visibility to the success rate of matching job seekers with jobs. Multiple attempts had been made to redefine the work and bring the talent development specialist or TDS (who worked with the job seekers) together with the business relationship representatives or BSR. The desire was to set up a workshop to improve the value stream and to make changes in each of the county offices. The goal was to efficiently move the job seekers through the value stream of finding a job. A scoping meeting was held to define the focus of a Lean value stream workshop.

After the initial Lean training of the leadership team, the team assembled to draft the scoping document. (See Figure 5.3) Two main resource groups were involved in the workshop session. The talent development specialist (who met regularly with the job seekers) needed to be brought together with the business services representatives (who spent most of their time with the businesses in the county) to define a common set of practices and procedures. The scoping document identified that various community nonprofits, career navigators, and representatives of veterans (suppliers) provided job referrals (inputs). The drawing in the middle (process) defined the high-level value stream by which the job applicants (output) were matched with the employers looking to fill jobs (customers). The team walked through the 5 steps of scoping:

SIPOC: suppliers, inputs, process, outputs, customer

| Project Name: Talent Development Spec to Business Solution Unit | Process Sponsor: Angie Barksdale | Date 12/21/2016 |
| VS Manager: Assistant Managers 1 and 2 | Project Manager: Tasha Evans | |

Objective:
Clearly state what has to be accomplished in the Workshop. Include measures.

Goals for Process Improvement:
1. Increase the number of jobs filled by employers by job seekers - doubled with monthly goal.
2. Track job seekers and jobs filled
3. The time to fill jobs is cut in half with monthly goals.
4. Understand and see progress on a weekly basis

1. Need to define a process to connect job seekers to with TDS
2. TDS is as knowledgeable and empowered as BSR (no trust issues)
3. TDS brings more value to the job seeker
4. Well defined job role & responsibilities and the same for all locations
5. TDS is fully trained and 6. Shared metrics between TDS and BSU

Suppliers:
Career Navigators
Veterans Representative
Community non profits

Customers: Employers in high demand industries (with openings)

START WITH — Current State: Value stream map (high level or list of process steps) — END WITH

Inputs:
Referrals

Outputs:
Talent Blast
Job Seeker application

Current Metrics:
Number of job seekers
Jobs filled
Retention rate
Employers served
Wages

IT Systems:
Spreadsheets listing employers and job seekers, by county

In Scope:

Out of Scope:
Job seekers who are not ready (with barriers or missing skills)

Issues & Problems:
1. Different reporting relationships.
2. TDS and BSU report into two different managers.
3. Differences exist in service center staffing
4. Different understandings in TDS Roles.
5. Little connection to BSU
6. TDS doesn't know BSU relationships
7. TDS as a rule doesn't connect to employers
8. Migrated from Kent county in Oct 2015 without clear definitions
9. Several attempts at redefining
10. Need to define which clients need TDS
11. Each employer has different application rules and processes
12. TDS is tired of waiting for BSU and has stopped using BSU
13. Wait time for BSU is too long
14. Some offices have TDS at front of process, others at end of process
15. TDS may or may not do a talent search
16. Need to be aware of TDS funding requirements
17. Career coach acts as TDS
18. We don't know how well the West Michigan Works! TDS process fills jobs
19. TDS needs more education
20. TDS needs empowerment

Workshop Participants:
TDS — Meanie Wolters (Muskegon), Deb Meniuc (Allegan), Jennifer VanVoorst (Ottawa), Roxanna Visser (Kent), Bashawn Robinson (Kent)
Career Navigator — Damila Meenigs, Ryan Nyamp
BSR — Michelle Brudevich (Allegan), Mike Blakley (Kent), Jayne Lindblom (Kent), Rory Crasco (Ottawa), Jared Schulte (Muskegon)
Coach — Heather Bates, Jennifer Henderson

Decision Panel participants:
Board Member (employer) from Talent Solution Committee (TBD)
Board Member (employee) from Business Solution Committee (TBD)
BSU Director - Deb
CEO - Angie Barksdale

Workshop and Decision Panel Dates:
Workshop Day 1: Feb 1 - 8:30 - 4:30
Decision Panel 1: Feb 2 at 3:30 pm
Workshop Day 2: Feb 2 - 8:30 - 4:30
Decision Panel 2: Decision Panel at 3:30 pm
DP day 30: Mar 2 - time TBD
DP day 60: Mar 30 - time TBD
DP day 90: April 27 - time TBD

Next Steps:
1. Schedule the Workshop (Feb 1 & 2 8:30 - 4:30 each day) with lunch
2. Name board members for decision panel
3. Schedule decision panel for workshop dates (Feb 1 3:30-4:30 and Feb 2 3:30 - 4:30)
4. Schedule decision panel follow-up for 30, 60 and 90 days.

FIGURE 5.3
SIPOC for an employment agency project.

Supplier – community nonprofits, career navigators, and representatives of veterans

Inputs – job referrals

Process – the high-level steps of the job referral process

Output – job applications

Customer – area employers

The high-level value stream with its work steps (shown described in the center of the scoping document) is not yet defined in enough detail to understand the entire value stream in sufficient detail, but the high-level view is intended to give direction to the discussion and to inform the goals and objectives for the workshop. Already at this stage of describing the value stream, there were no shortages of problems identified by the leadership team with the existing work methods. A total of 20 problems were quickly listed by the leadership team.

Six goals were defined for the workshop during the scoping event:

1. Define a method to connect job seekers with a talent development specialist (TDS).
2. Make sure the TDS is as knowledgeable and empowered as the business solutions representatives (BSR) (no trust issues).
3. Ensure that TDS brings more value to the job seeker.
4. Have well-defined job roles and responsibilities for all locations.
5. Ensure TDS is fully trained.
6. Share metrics between TDS and BSU.

The goals describe the intent of the workshop session. If these goals are accomplished, then the work will flow better and the people in the value stream will be more successful. Goals can be general and point the team in a direction. The goals inform the objectives of the workshop.

The objectives are meant to be challenging and aspirational. Each one describes something that didn't exist in the current work.

1. Increase the number of jobs filled by employers with job seekers – with a measurable metric to double the number of jobs filled to be tracked with a monthly measure against the goal.
2. Track job seekers and jobs filled.
3. The time to fill jobs is cut in half with monthly goals.
4. Understand and see progress on a weekly basis.

The objectives are indeed measurable, one of the tests of a good objective. Each objective has a specific value to move: double the jobs filled, cut the time in half, and see the progress on a weekly basis. The 50% rule of improvement is evident in these objectives.

The scoping document also defined what was in scope or out of scope for the workshop. For this workshop, it was decided that the effort of getting job seekers ready to enter the job search was out of scope. It was recognized as an effort for another workshop in the future. Taking that initiative off the table brought the scope for the current value stream mapping project to a manageable size.

The workshop brought together a team of 14 people from the 5 county offices. Each one had an individual view of the value stream and opinions of how the work should flow. Angie Barksdale noted, "The workshop brought to light some major philosophical differences between the counties and between the departments." The scoping session was held just before Christmas of 2016, and the workshop was scheduled about 6 weeks out in February of 2017. The team was assembled in one of the 5 county offices and worked through the current state, its problems, and opportunities. A future state vision was created for a standard method across the 5 county offices.

One of the kaizens identified was to have a visual board that tracked the job seekers and employer opportunities. By using the board, the team could track the job seekers' progress in finding work. The team could track the amount of time each job seeker was on the board and when he or she should come off the visual display board.

The two functions (the talent development specialist and business services representatives) currently meet twice per week at the visual boards to discuss opportunities and job seeker/opportunity fit. Each county uses the same visual board and the same methods, so the value stream is now standardized across all the 5 county offices.

The teams report to an organization metric on their common website. The metric reports the total number of jobs filled and the number of employers served with potential candidates. With numbers in the hundreds, it is encouraging for entire organization to see this metric every time they log onto their internal website. Prior to the workshop and the improvements, they did not have visuals on how they were reaching their goals of filling the jobs and then number of employers served.

The team presented its Lean improvements and success at a state-wide gathering of similar agencies. It received a good deal of interest in the improved value stream, and serval other county offices from other parts of the state came to the West Michigan Works! offices to learn how the teams applied Lean principles to improve their job seeker success rate through the application of value stream mapping in a workshop setting.

SUMMARY

The One Main Thing – Scoping for the value stream mapping session with the stakeholders and leaders gives focus and direction for the upcoming workshop and its participants.

STUDY QUESTIONS

1. What are the six steps of the value stream mapping method?
2. Who attends the scoping sessions?
3. What are the key roles identified on the scoping document? What does each one do?
4. What does an ideal workshop team look like?
5. What is the difference between the goals and objectives on the scoping document?
6. What is the purpose of homework prior to the value stream workshop session?

6

The Anatomy of a Value Stream Mapping Workshop

Lean is all about continuous improvement of the organization's value stream. Office value streams can be improved one small step at a time; however, often the value stream requires a complete overhaul. Transformation at the value stream level requires looking at the complete end-to-end process steps, observing the wastes in and between those steps, and looking for large-scale improvements in that value stream. Change at this level requires innovation across the departments in the value stream, but it also requires making the value streams visible so the wastes can be identified. The challenge is to expose the value stream, which remains nearly completely hidden from view, residing in computers, email, and other work systems.

In manufacturing, the operational value streams and the flow of products through the build and assembly operators are directly observable. If you stand on the manufacturing floor and watch the products as the workers build them, you will see physical items moving through the plant and motion of the operators. You will see where there is flow of parts, and where flow is missing. Where there is a lack of flow, wastes will be obvious, and there will be inventory build-up, which should be relatively easy to spot. The inventory will be evident as parts stored in bins or racks. When the operators are constantly moving, looking for tools, parts, and paper work, then there is the waste of excess motion. Defects and rework can be observed in the unfinished parts or sub-assemblies that are set aside for inspection and corrective action. These visible wastes and flow problems become the targets of kaizen efforts on the factory floor.

THE CHALLENGE OF THE OFFICE VALUE STREAM

Once the lens of Lean is moved from the manufacturing areas to the office, the ability to see value streams or detect flow of information (or lack thereof) becomes very difficult. On the office side of the concrete wall, the work steps are hidden from view. Everyone appears quite busy at their desk, intently looking at computer screens, clicking the keys of the keyboards. What anyone is actually working on, however, is not discernable. With the work and information flow so hidden, it is difficult to even know where to shine the light on the value stream to target areas for improvements. If that in itself doesn't create enough obfuscation, the handoffs of the work are not seen either. The information flow can be buried in a couple of ways. The movement of information from one person to another occurs through email or the inner workings of the IT systems. In these cases, the actually knowledge of the inner workings of the value stream might only fully be known by the information technology professional who created the systems. In other cases, the information transformation is completed only by email.

To make matters worse, the work steps performed by knowledge workers often are not fully documented. In too many cases, the understanding of what to do with the work once it arrives on the desktop is only known in the heads of the knowledge workers. The "tribal knowledge" exists as long as the people are in their jobs. If they go on vacation, are transferred, or worse – leave the company – then the knowledge of how to do the work leaves with them.

The work in the office is rarely looked at in its entirety, across its value stream. Without an overall value stream focus, improvements over time only happen at the department level, and the value stream as a whole is never considered. Work processes are sub-optimized at the department level, and the changes made are, at best, Band Aids on the overall value stream. The best course of action is to rip off the Band Aids to expose the underlying problems in the value stream and to help the organization work toward eliminating wastes and regain efficiencies.

Enter the value stream mapping workshop. The purpose of mapping the value streams in the office is to take a holistic view of the value stream to reduce inefficiencies and make improvements. The goal is to rapidly analyze and transform the value streams of the organization. This can occur with more speed than one might imagine.

The three reasons to map the value stream are

- to make the work visible,
- to point to problems, and
- to focus on making improvements.

This trifecta of the value stream mapping methodology is accomplished by mapping the work that is hidden with mapping symbols.

WHAT TO MAP?

Every organization contains a number of value streams that are central to its existence. There are most likely a few critical value streams that are central to how an organization functions, and in a large organization there are many smaller streams between departments. In a medium to large organization, there could be 50 to 100 sub-processes. All of these should be mapped.

After selecting which value stream to map, an initial first step is to understand what actually flows through the value. The information or services that satisfy the customer should be identified and guide the mapping process. Whenever possible, I like to put emphasis on the actual customer and how the value stream serves him or her. Think of what the end customer (or client) receives from the value stream and then follow that flow through the work stream. The goal is to provide the best value for the customer with the least amount of effort and waste.

The focus of the value stream is always the end user or customer, as shown in Figure 6.1 For instance, a service provider for a loan would consider the loan documents moving through value stream from the point of view of the borrower. An insurance company would map the claims as they move through the work steps from the point of view of the policyholder. The HR department would consider the candidate as she or he moves through the on-boarding process. A college might map the application process from the point of view of the student. A non-profit would map the service it provides from the point of view of the client.

Having the voice of the end user or customer in the mapping session is an effective technique to ensure that needs are properly considered.

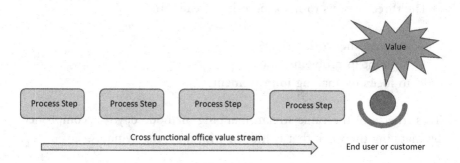

FIGURE 6.1
Cross-functional value streams serve the end customer.

The end user will be willing to share an actual experience, both the good and the bad, and help to uncover the wastes, quality issues, rework, and other inefficiencies. If the map is being done at a lower level (compared to the overall value stream), and the end user or customer is not immediately evident, the next receiving process inside the organization becomes the customer. In these cases, the customer is internal to the organization.

In Chapter 2, the wastes of office work were described in detail. The opportunities for improvements were also explored. There are typically so many wastes and inefficiencies, that the opportunity for improvements is significant. At the time of launching a Lean value stream mapping initiative, if the improvement targets are unclear, the team can assume the "rule of 50%." That is to say, the team should attempt to remove 50% of the wastes. Figure 6.2 shows how the 50% improvement goal translates to a 50% reduction in work steps, total cycle time, handoffs, and any rework due to processing errors.

The metrics for the success of the workshop directly follow the 50% improvement targets.

COMPARE THE CURRENT AND FUTURE STATES TO HIGHLIGHT THE IMPROVEMENT

A good future state map will show the comparison between the current state and the future state. Several different measures are

Goals for Office Value Stream Mapping Initiatives

• 50% reduction in process steps
• 50% reduction in total cycle time
• 50% reduction in hand-offs
• 50% reduction in errors, rework

FIGURE 6.2
Goals for office value stream mapping initiatives.

compared to show the contrast. The goal for the improvements can be double checked at this juncture. Each measure is listed and posted next to the future state map, using a table similar to the one shown in Table 6.1. The goal is to show the contrast in before and after measurements.

FITTING VALUES STREAM MAPPING INTO BUSY PEOPLE'S SCHEDULES

Office value streams are in as much need of overhaul as are those in manufacturing. In manufacturing, one-week kaizens are often used, and workers are pulled from production to work on process improvements. However, that model does not work in the office. In a manufacturing plant, the equipment can be moved in a week, workers can be retrained, and documentation is updated. Sometimes rapid equipment moves and changes to the workflow are done overnight, during a weekend, a long holiday weekend, or a plant shut down. This is not always possible in the office. Complex office improvement activities require more time to change. In many instances, information system changes are required; these take time to design, change, and implement. The fact the office value streams are highly interconnected means that they need to be looked at holistically. The individual steps are difficult to change without looking at how they fit together. *The goal of the office value stream mapping exercise is to transform the process holistically.* This takes time,

TABLE 6.1

Current State and Future State Value Stream Mapping Metrics

Measure	Current State	Future State	Improvement
Total cycle time			
Total processing time			
Number of steps			
First time quality			

and it is logistically difficult to pull office workers from their regular jobs for even a week to look at things in a holistic way.

Often in the office, the workers are the only ones who do their particular jobs, and it is difficult to have someone cover or back-fill for them. They have specialized skills and knowledge that they alone have mastered. The prospect of cross-training another person to be able to cover for them for a week or longer is unfeasible and impractical. Pulling the knowledge workers from their regular jobs for a whole week would cause the work to seriously stall or derail. It is not uncommon to find office workers who are stretched to their limits, and convincing them or their supervisors to take a week or more to re-engineer the way they work generates skepticism. They will ask, "How is the work going to get done while we are pulled away trying to change the way we work?"

THE OFFICE VALUE STREAM MAPPING WORKSHOP MODEL

The overall value stream workshop model is shown in Figure 6.3. The model moves sequentially through the steps of defining the scope with the leadership, walking the process (Gemba), drawing the current state and future state, defining the process improvements, and finally, implementing the kaizen plan. The office workshop model involves thoroughly preparing for the value stream mapping session, the workshop facilitator scopes with leaders and Gemba walks the work steps. The workshop itself is a 1- to 3-day event, but that is followed by a 30- to 90-day implementation phase. During the implementation phase, the knowledge workers can return to their

Lean Workshop Format

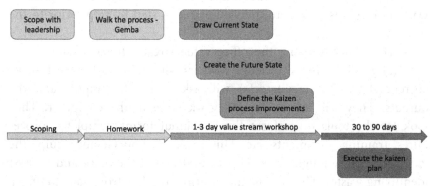

FIGURE 6.3
The high-level workshop method.

work, but they will still be asked to participate in the improvement kaizens for a few hours a week.

In nearly all cases, a 3-day value stream mapping workshop is enough time to map a complex office value stream, including the current state map, the future state map, and the initial plans for the improvement efforts. The improvement ideas and plans are captured in a series of kaizen A3 documents.

Chapter 5 laid the important groundwork of scoping the Lean workshop and putting all of the players in the room together. The goal is to get a clear view of the entire value stream, at a level of detail that allows the team to suggest meaningful improvements. Figure 6.1 shows the overall workshop model. Here we will assume that the first three steps of contracting, scoping, and Lean training have been completed.

WALKING THE FLOW OF THE WORK AND THE INFORMATION

Manufacturing Lean emphasizes Gemba, or going to the place where something is done and looking for the problem within the manufacturing value stream. This involves going to the factory floor. When Lean is applied to the office, the same concept applies, but a different technique is required. Earlier in the chapter, we established that much of the work in the office is hidden, and the goal of the workshop is to make the office value stream transparent. The primary way to do this is "walk" to the value stream, step by step, prior to the workshop.

When Gemba walking the office value stream, the workshop facilitator(s) go(es) to the knowledge workers who perform the work in its current state. The facilitator(s) will ask to see the inputs and the outputs. They will ask to see the work done in the computer. They look for the tools to perform the job: input forms, templates, procedures, training documents, etc. This pre-workshop Gemba equips the facilitator with enough knowledge to understand the work and to start identifying wastes. They follow the information flow from start to finish. They are interested in how the work is received, how it is modified, and what signifies that it is ready to move on to the next step in the process. While walking the office value stream step by step, they observe and interview office workers, taking notes and making observations as to where the work steps might be in need of fixing. Their notebooks are full of documented wastes. As the steps in the value stream start to take shape, the sketches in their notebooks start to resemble preliminary sketches of the steps in the value stream.

CURRENT STATE MAPPING

Armed with the homework, the facilitators assemble with the workshop team in a conference room with a large whiteboard. These knowledge workers were identified in the scoping session and were part of the Gemba-walking homework. This is the first time that many of the participants will see the value stream laid out end to end. I am often surprised to learn that this is the first time that some of them have even met each other, having previously only communicated via email or phone. While this might not be true in smaller organizations, it is very true in nearly every large organization.

The 1- to 3-day workshop has three major steps: drawing the current state map, designing the future state, and defining the kaizen improvement efforts that will be needed to transform the value stream into an improved future state. Each of these is broken down in further detail in Figure 6.4.

Current State Mapping

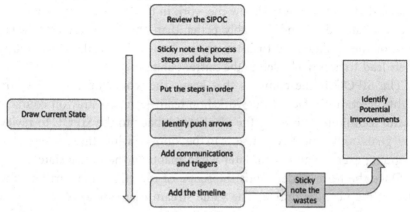

FIGURE 6.4
Diagram of the steps to map the current state.

The first item on the workshop agenda is to review the SIPOC with the team. This document should have been sent out beforehand, but it deserves a review by the team since it is the governing document for the workshop. The goals and objectives on this document should be a compass to the workshop team during the entire session to maintain the proper direction and focus on the desired objectives for the future state value stream. The SIPOC also lays out what is in and out of scope, and this typically becomes a topic of discussion. The facilitators can ask for clarifications on the SIPOC from the workshop team, but they should hold the team steady to the directional intent of the goals and objective in the SIPOC, which were documented by the value stream leaders during the scoping session.

On occasion, the team will challenge the scope of the workshop as stated in the SIPOC. In one situation, the team kept telling me in a value stream mapping workshop that we had to move further up in the value stream. I was being a little stubborn in this case, and I was holding them to the original scope. One woman in particular was insistent that we consider the work steps that occurred earlier in the value stream. I held firm, and so did she. It turned out that she was right. The steps up front that I thought were out of scope were indeed important steps to consider, and, in fact, we could not move forward to adopt a new future state without including those steps in the map. The lesson here is that the knowledge workers always know the work in the value stream better than the facilitator does and probably better than their own leadership. The goal of the facilitator is to listen to the knowledge workers and follow their lead to accurately define the current state map.

The SIPOC is the compass that keeps the workshop pointed in the right direction. In fact, if the workshop team seems to stray off course, a useful technique is to bring the whole team back to the SIPOC to review the goals and objectives. This can be done during the current state mapping exercise and again later when mapping the future state.

Once the team understands the scope of the effort, the current value stream map can be drawn. The value stream mapping symbols become the standard language in the organization for describing all value streams. Any value stream can be mapped and can be quickly understood with just a few symbols.

When I first facilitated workshop teams, I drew the map while the participants explained the work steps to me. This turned out to be a very inefficient method. The whole room waited (which is a waste) for each other to describe their step in the process, and the conversation had to proceed one person at a time. A much more efficient method was to have them write down their own work individually and then share it. Each knowledge worker is asked to write down the process steps for which he or she is responsible in the process, using a drawing of the process box on one sticky note and a data box on another sticky note, as shown in Figure 6.5. With some basic instructions, the knowledge workers can easily fill these out. The added benefit of using sticky notes is that when the actual value stream map is created, the sticky notes can easily be moved.

The instructions for the process box are to write the process step with a verb and a noun. The body of the sticky note contains more detail of the work that is done to transform the information. In the lower right-hand corner, the technology (or information system) used for the process step is listed.

The data box needs a little more definition. The lower sticky in Figure 6.4 shows the data box and typically the details that are captured. Often in the workshop, the processing time, cycle time, and percent complete and accurate are not known. However, the knowledge workers do the work and can easily estimate these. In the office, the work has

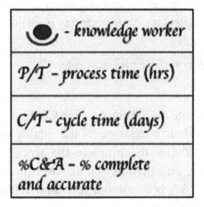

FIGURE 6.5
Mapping symbols – process box and data box.

varying levels of complexity; allowing the knowledge workers to reflect on the variation in their estimating is always a good idea.

Data box icon definition:

The knowledge worker is given by name. If this is an individual, typically a first name and last initial is used. (e.g., Mary S.). However, if a group of people performs the process step, then the name of the group is given with the number of individuals in that group (e.g., Order Dept. – 3)

P/T – processing time (hrs.)

The processing time, or P/T, is the amount of time it requires to do a task. Processing time is often referred to as "heads down time" or "time on the keyboard." This time is typically measured in minutes to hours.

C/T – cycle time (days – weeks)

The cycle time, or C/T, is the elapsed time to complete the step. It represents the time it takes to complete the task once it reaches the person doing the work. It is typically measured in days, and the unit of time is days. If it spans multiple days, an 8-hour day is assumed to be the norm.

%C&A – percent complete and accurate

The percent complete and accurate, or %C&A, is a value given to the incoming quality. This is a measure of the quality of the work coming in and reflects the ability to complete the work that comes to that processing step. If the information that arrives is incomplete, or requires rework, then the %C&A is a number less than 100%. It is not uncommon for the incoming quality to be quite low.

Those familiar with mapping manufacturing will recognize that the quality measure in the office value stream is different from the quality metric in manufacturing). In manufacturing, the out-going quality of each work step is accounted for, with the goal of measuring first pass yield of all of the steps in the value stream. However, in the office, the worker often corrects the information when processing the work to remove defects. Therefore, the incoming quality, tracked as a percentage of complete and accurate, is a better measure.

W/T – wait time (days – weeks)

The wait time, or W/T, is not included in the data box for the reason that it is the time that the work spends waiting to start the process step.

It is the time just ahead of the process step, and it represents idle time in the value stream. An icon of a clock is used to indicate wait time. If there is wait time, there is typically inventory as well. On the office value stream the wait time is indicated with the icon of an "inbox" (Again, those familiar with mapping manufacturing value streams will recognize that inventory is represented with a Triangle with an "I" in the center. In office maps, we indicated that the inventory is sitting in either a physical in tray or a virtual one in the computer.

Inventory is shown with an inbox and wait time with a clock.

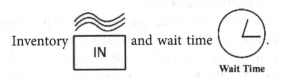

Other important icons show the movement of information. Since most processing happens by a form of push (such as a physical handoff between workers or with email), the most common connection between the process steps is represented with a push arrow.

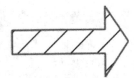

Additional icons for mapping current states show the ways steps are triggered to start. Information will come into the step either via a manual method (paper) or via an electronic method (email, FAX, workflow, etc.).

Incoming information:

Manual:———————————————————▶

Electronic:————⌐ˍ———▶

The mapping value stream follows a repeatable pattern.

1. The participants write down their work steps using a process box and a data box.
2. The participants are asked to place them on a white board in order of their sequence.

3. The facilitator walks through the steps with the group. Each sticky note is read, and the work steps are discussed. The facilitator stops to add additional symbols as needed between the steps (push arrows, inventory, wait time, information flow arrows). See Figure 6.6 for an example of a value stream map using a combination of sticky notes and symbols.

4. The workshop team typically finds they have not fully described the work, and the facilitator asks them for additional detail and writes it on the sticky notes. It is not uncommon for the team to realize that steps have been omitted, and the facilitator asks the individuals to add these to the map with additional sticky notes.

5. The facilitator asks the participants to document any issues or problems with a different color sticky note. These are the wastes in the process.

6. At the end of the mapping, the facilitator adds a timeline to the bottom with the team. See the hand drawn value stream map in Figure 6.6 for an example of a value stream map with a timeline at the bottom. It is common for the team to start to add their initial kaizen "burst" ideas to a map as shown in Figure 6.7.

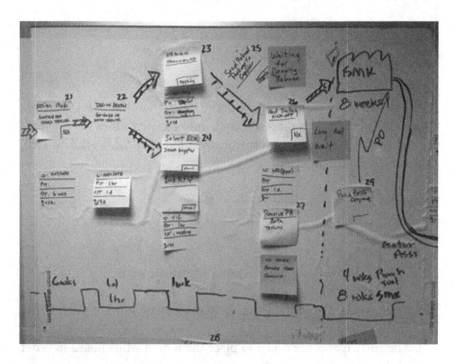

FIGURE 6.6
A portion of a current state value stream map done in a workshop.

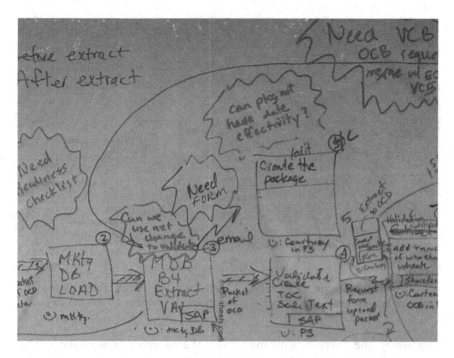

FIGURE 6.7
Hand-drawn current state map using process boxes, data boxes, push arrows and initial kaizen bursts for improvement ideas.

It is not uncommon for the maps to get very large and messy depending on the complexity of the value stream.

A large complete current state like the one shown in Figure 6.8 would take a whole day to complete. Once the current state map is captured, the facilitator will ask the team for ideas for improvements. A helpful technique is to review the sticky notes that describe the problems and the wastes in the value stream. The goal is to capture the initial thoughts and ideas on how to fix the major problems.

FUTURE STATE MAPPING

Once the team has generated the current state map, it is ready to tackle the future state design. This stage of the method requires some guidance from the Lean facilitator. The team will already have some ideas on

FIGURE 6.8
A workshop team is mapping a complex current state value stream. The workshop facilitator and the team listen as one of the participants describes the process steps.

improving the current state map from the prior day's workshop. The facilitator points out the wastes and introduces ideas on ways to make the work flow with less interruptions, less wastes, and increased quality.

MOVING TO THE FUTURE STATE REQUIRES INNOVATION

I have heard the claim that Lean and innovation are at odds. These pundits claim that Lean's emphasis on standard work and documentation seems opposed to innovation techniques. "Lean is a structured approach, but innovation is unstructured," goes the argument. However, in reality the opposite is true. Moving from a current state to future state requires a high degree of innovation. The workshop team innovates when it transforms a current state value stream mapping into a new system that eliminates wastes and creates flow.

REVIEW LEAN PRINCIPLES

The workshop facilitator guides the team through the steps shown in Figure 6.9, starting with a review of the Lean principles. The facilitator

Future State Mapping

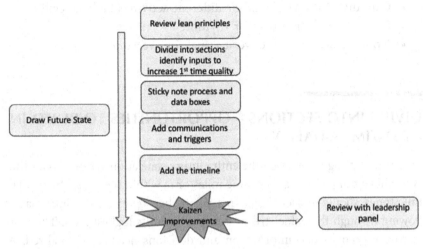

FIGURE 6.9
Future state mapping diagram.

reminds the participants of the basic Lean concepts surrounding flow. The future state map should seek to replace push with pull. In a push system, the work is sent to the downstream step whether it is ready for it or not. Email is always a push system. The future state should attempt to flow the work or to create a pull method to transfer work from one step to another. Many forms of pull systems can be used. Table 2.4 in Chapter 2 listed many of the ideas for achieving pull in the value stream.

A series of questions can be used to help the workshop team put the customer first in the value stream. When these are placed in front of the workshop team, it will have a better chance of designing a future state that will be a Lean system. These were documented by Drew Locher and Beau Keyte from their book *The Complete Lean Enterprise*, and they can be used as a guide during the future state redesign of the value stream.

- What does the customer value?
- Which steps create value, and which are waste?
- Challenge every step: Are there activities we can just stop doing?
- How can we flow the work with fewer interruptions?
- Are the steps in the right sequence?

- How will the work be prioritized?
- Are there resource issues causing bottlenecks?
- Can any of the workload or different activities be balanced?
- Can we establish a pace or rhythm?
- How can we make the work visual for everyone?

DIVIDE INTO SECTIONS – OPPORTUNITIES TO BUILD IN FIRST-TIME QUALITY

Often attempting to redesign the entire future state at once can be daunting. A useful technique is to select some milestones within the value stream. The milestones should reflect the points when the quality of the information flowing through the value stream needs to be at its highest level. These are often the points when information and decisions need to be finalized. At these junctures, draw a vertical line and list the inputs that should be completed with the highest quality, and then work backwards from that section. These intermediate goals will allow the workshop team to redefine the value stream in sections.

STICKY NOTE THE FUTURE STATE

The new future state value stream can be drafted with sticky notes just as the current state map was. Use sticky notes for process steps and for the kaizens. Anytime there is a new step, or when there is an improvement that needs to be made to an existing step, a kaizen burst is added to the map. It is not uncommon in some parts of the map to have as many improvements, or kaizen bursts, as process steps. You will also notice that there are clusters of improvements around parts of the value stream that require the most modifications. Kaizens are the high-level solutions to the problems that were identified on the current state map. Each kaizen represents a change or innovation to the map. Later in the workshop method, these will be prioritized and put in order of sequence for implementation. At this point in the workshop, it is most important to capture the essence of these ideas from the team in sufficient detail that the facilitator and the team will be able to recall the essence of the idea. Figure 6.10 shows a segment of a future state map design to transform a value stream with a number of kaizens.

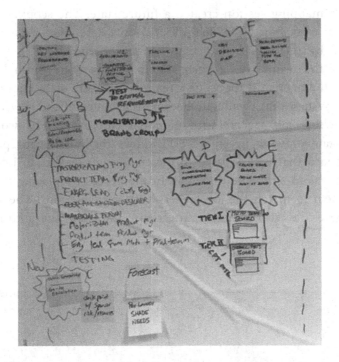

FIGURE 6.10

The beginning drawing of a future state map with kaizens A through F which will transform the value stream map. It is not uncommon for the Kaizens to outnumber the work steps on a future state value stream map.

DEFINE NEW COMMUNICATION PATHS AND INFORMATION FLOW

As the future state map unfolds, all of the new communication paths and information flows that drive the information flow should be added to the map. These are shown with the same mapping symbols that were used in the current state map. The critical difference is to ensure that the push scenarios are replaced by information pull methods whenever possible. The visual board, or virtual list, that eventually will be used to ensure pull can be drawn on the future state map. The drawing on the future state map will be a prototype of the one that is eventually used on the actual map.

The case study at the end of Chapter 5 introduced us to the scoping session for West MichiganWorks! Let's take a closer look at how this mapping session created a future state. The scoping session led to a workshop in which the current state map was created, followed by the future state map on the second day. The current state for the teams was a push system mostly done through email between the people in the value stream. The future state map defined the pull system that eventually became the center of the new method for matching job seekers with potential employers. The workshop future state drawing in Figure 6.11 shows the initial concepts of a visual board that will be used to match the job seekers to jobs. The concept was to eliminate the email in the process, replacing it with a pull system to match the job seekers with available jobs. The kaizens to achieve the visual system are also shown on the future state drawing.

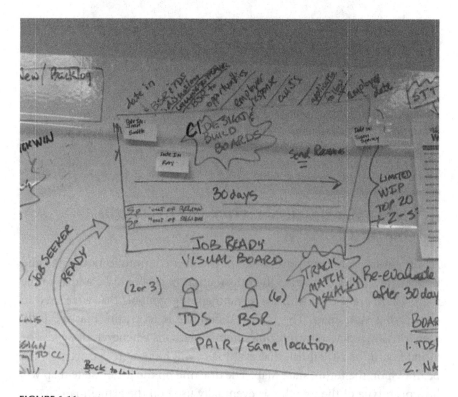

FIGURE 6.11
Initial concepts of the pull system. The future state map had the first crude prototype drawing of the visual board that would eventually become the pull system of the future state.

This initial rough workshop prototype gave enough of an image of how the final board would look. The workshop kaizen team used the initial sketch to create a visual board for the teams. Eventually, the completed boards would become the standard across 5 offices in separate counties. Today, the staff uses the boards to match job seekers with employers. The metric of the number of people hired per month became the measure of success in the final system as well.

In the future state "pull" system, both the talent development specialist (TDS) and the business solutions representative (BSR) meet at the board in a stand-up meeting, as seen in Figure 6.12. In the meeting, they look at the job seekers who are ready to apply for work and match them to employees.

FIGURE 6.12
The final pull system. This was first imagined in the workshop future state.

IDENTIFY KAIZENS IMPROVEMENTS – "GOOD CHANGES" TO THE VALUE STREAM

All the kaizens needed to create the future state are included in a list of changes to be made. Once they are identified, the team will be asked to identify them in more detail. For the initial kaizen capture, a simple, large, poster-size sheet of paper will capture the kaizen outputs from the workshop. The 90-day rule is applied, to complete the kaizens in the first 90 days of implementation. The solutions will certainly be perfected more in the future as the team learns what works and what doesn't work. Minor IT system changes such as adding a field or changing a report are included; however, the 90-day window generally excludes any major IT system changes. The challenge to the team is to find a low-tech method that can be used, in the first 90 days to change the value stream. The facilitator describes, "Make the process change first, and then automate" and then adds emphasis by saying, "Use creativity before capital." If a kaizen will take longer than 90 days, then it is labeled as "future," and its impact on moving to the future state is minimize by doing other things.

The kaizens are given a little more detail at this stage than just a kaizen burst on the map. The team must define the actual problem it is solving and how it believes the problem will be solved and by whom. Table 6.2 shows a format that can be used within the workshop to outline the kaizens that need to be completed to achieve the future state.

TABLE 6.2

Kaizen Detailed Plan

Kaizen Letter (A, B, C, D)
Kaizen name
Kaizen description/problem being solved
Owner *(name)*
Support *(names)*
Tasks *(list)*
Target date for completion *(date)*
Degree of complexity/effort *(easy, medium, difficult)*

The kaizen owner is identified and almost always is a member of the workshop team. The owner should not be assigned to someone outside the room unless there is a prior agreement that this person can take on the task. At this stage of the kaizen definition we say, "There can be no blind assigning of kaizens." The support names are of the people who will help get the tasks done. The kaizen owner may not have any tasks at all on the list. Instead, he or she is coordinating the kaizen activity with the support people. The kaizen owner will also report out weekly to the workshop project manager.

Quick Wins

The facilitator always looks for what I call the quick-win kaizens. These are the kaizens that are suggested during the workshop and can be done in a few hours. In some cases, these changes can be made within the workshop itself. These are fun because they motivate the team and give it a sense of accomplishment and confidence as it moves forward, for example, simple IT system changes or new reports are often easily done during the workshop or immediately after and would classified as "quick wins." In one workshop, the team identified a simple IT system change that would eliminate a manual step in the work. The team talked about it in the workshop and outlined the requirement. The next day, the IT team member showed the team the field that was added to the system overnight that the team could start using right away. These give the team momentum for moving forward with the rest of the changes.

LEADERSHIP PANEL PREPARATION AND REVIEW

The leadership team is brought into the workshop at the end of the future state section. At this point, the team has drawn the current state map and the future state map and has listed out the kaizens. The goal is to gain alignment with the leaders before moving forward with more detailed planning.

The leadership panel is made up of the stakeholders.

The facilitator spends a few minutes with the panel just prior to the report-out. The goal is to alert the panel to its responsibilities as it listens to the team report out. The talking points with the leadership panel go something like this:

- What were the challenges the team faced?
- Were there any problem participants, and how was the situation managed?
- Please listen and ask questions of clarification, but let the team finish presenting.
- After the future state and kaizens are presented, please give your reaction.
- Look for things the team might have missed.
- Be bolder and more ambitious if required.
- Give the recommendations for modifying the map if needed.
- Endorse the team to proceed with the kaizen planning.

While the facilitator is preparing the leadership panel, the team is preparing its presentation to the leaders. The facilitator tells the team during the workshop that it will be presenting to the leadership panel. This is done for the very important reason that the goal is for the team to own the value stream. It is too easy for this to be placed back on the facilitator. So, the facilitator has to actively work to give ownership to the team. In fact, it is always a good idea for the facilitator to give control to the team while the future state map is being drawn. This is called "giving them the marker." There is often a point in a future state mapping exercise when the facilitator knows that the team has taken ownership, and it is at the point when someone from the team gets up and explains his or her idea for the future state and takes the marker and starts drawing on the map.

The typical agenda for the future state mapping exercise is shown in Table 6.3. It is best to give each agenda item to a different team member to ensure that everyone gets a chance to present to the leadership panel. One member of the workshop should be assigned the task of capturing the comments from the leadership. These will be used during the debrief, after the leaders have left the room. More often than not the workshop team will adjust its future state map after the leaders give their comments.

Some teams will have fun with the workshop report-out, even performing a skit of the work methods before and after the planned changes.

TABLE 6.3

Workshop Kaizen Report-Out

Introduction of the Team and Leaders (5 min.)	All
Current state map review (10 min.)	*Workshop team member*
Review of problems (5 min.)	*Workshop team member*
Future state map review (15 min.)	*Workshop team member*
Kaizens and owners (10 min.)	*Workshop team member*
Discussion (15 min.)	*All*

KAIZEN PLANNING

Up to this point, the kaizens are not estimated very accurately but are placed in three categories: 0–30 days, 31–60 days, and 61–90 days. The desired outcome is to find the quick wins and the longer-term initiatives and to present these to the leadership panel to gain their agreement. The 90-day plan is the optimal timeframe for completing kaizens in the office. Why 90-days? In most organizations, getting something done in 90 days is lightning fast! Anything too much longer than the 90-day plan starts to drag out and become too undefined to be actionable. The project plan A3 is the tool used to show the 90-day plan. This summary document gives the current state and the future state and outlines the kaizens that are needed to achieve the future state. The 90-day plan is the governing document going forward. This is the same A3 style-reporting document used for documenting the kaizens in manufacturing, as described by David Mann (See Appendix A, Template D).

The A3s are written on the last day of the workshop. In this working session, the kaizen owners are asked to meet with their support people to define a more complete list of tasks for the kaizen and create a detailed weekly plan. These become the marching orders for the team to begin work on the kaizens. The leadership panel is asked to come in one more time to review the A3 plans. Each kaizen owner is asked to review the A3 project plan with the leaders.

After the workshop, the kaizen owners will continue to meet to discuss progress made on the plans. The plans should be displayed in a team space or common area since it will be regularly updated and reviewed by the leadership panel. For larger efforts, the A3 plan is broken into multiple A3s, and each one is tracked and updated by its owner.

WILL YOU EVER BE DONE MAPPING?

The office model is more successful if the kaizens are kicked off immediately after the workshop. On the last day of the workshop, the kaizens are placed in an implementation plan. During the 90-day effort, the team stays together to participate in the kaizens that will transform the value stream. Since the effort is spread across multiple weeks, a level of management of the workshop and following implementation is needed.

In reality, you are never done. The future state gives the direction to improve the value stream for the next 90 days or so. Once the kaizens are completed, the future state becomes the next current state.

CASE STUDY – HABITAT FOR HUMANITY OF KENT COUNTY

Habitat for Humanity of Kent County provides affordable homeownership opportunities for families in the city of Grand Rapids, Michigan, and surrounding communities. The connection between Habitat Kent and Steelcase was made through Mark Greiner, a Steelcase executive who also sits on the Board of Directors for Habitat Kent. Steelcase has been a longtime supporter of Habitat Kent, and when Greiner asked us to work with them to provide Lean improvements, my Lean buddy Jon VanSweden and I were excited to become involved.

Brandyn Deckinga, the director of construction services, was a quick student of Lean, and he quickly involved his team in Lean improvements. The team decided to tackle the bid value stream. Deckinga saw evidence of wastes and plenty of room for improvement. He observed too many handoffs, a lot of paper, and too many touch points. The workshop included Brandyn, Jason Parsons (project manager), Melody

Geerlings (construction coordinator), 2 other project managers, and 3 site supervisors. The warehouse manager, Tom Poll, who handled "gifts in kind" of materials and services also attended.

The bid process involves seeking bids from trades for jobs the volunteers are not qualified to perform. The trades help on construction jobs such as excavation, concrete, MEP-Mechanical, electrical, plumbing, roofing, drywall, and other jobs that require a professional. The challenge, per Deckinga, was that Habitat Kent competes with all new home construction in the area for the same trades, and this challenge is compounded because the Habitat model is to provide low-cost housing for families who otherwise would not be able to afford a new or renovated home. Habitat Kent has to compete for the trades without being able to pay a premium.

The Habitat Kent team worked through a value stream mapping session by looking at the work from end to end for the first time. They saw a process that had evolved over many iterations into one that had become overly complex with added overhead, unneeded steps, and extra touches. Deckinga described the existing methods as an "old school," paper-based process based on various grant requirements over the years. The paper-based process, and its wastes, were shown in the form of a current state map (see Figure 6.13). For each housing project, all of the materials required for the trades were printed and the trade bidders had to come to an open house for each project. The trades came into Habitat Kent to pick up the bid package. They returned signed copies of the paper-based bid packages. Habitat Kent staff kept all of the paper copies in notebooks that are mainly needed in the case of audits by various government funding sources. The funding requirements include tracking of the bid costs as well as the supplier that was awarded the project.

The difficulty was getting the trade people to come to the open house. The trades are in high demand, and Habitat Kent only had a 66% success rate in having them come in for an open house. Deckinga pointed out, "The trades are all really busy people. Many of them are small business owners. They needed something more convenient than attending open houses for every project."

During the workshop the team drew a future state map (see Figure 6.14), which included several kaizen improvement ideas. For instance, the team proposed an idea to make it easier to attract additional trades to the projects. Here the challenge is that Habitat

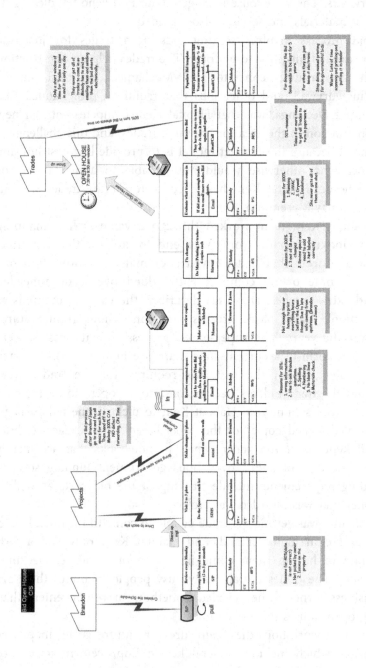

FIGURE 6.13

Case study: bid-spec current state. This map of the process at Habitat for Humanity of Kent County was recreated from the original hand-drawn value stream map. The yellow stickers represent problems in the work steps or between the steps.

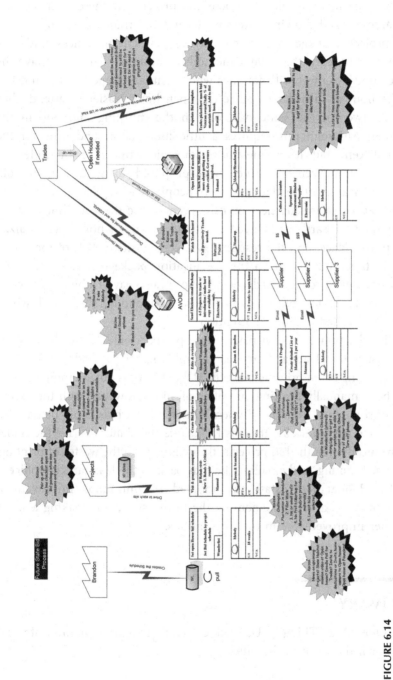

FIGURE 6.14

Case study: value stream future state map. Notice the kaizen bursts for potential improvements.

Kent competes for trades in the same market as all new home and remodel construction. The open houses provide a way for Habitat Kent to share its mission and the upcoming project. At these open houses, the architectural drawings are shared, and the tradespeople meet with the project manager to review any special circumstances with the project or to learn the habitat methods of building. They also have the opportunity to meet with families who eventually hope to own and live in the houses. In order to make the open house easier to attend, they created two on the same day, one in the morning and one in the evening. Although this requires a little more effort and time for the Habitat Kent staff, it provides more convenient times for the trades.

A key improvement kaizen was proposed to send out the bid packages via email so that the tradespeople who regularly placed bids could return their bids electronically even before the open house. They wouldn't necessarily even need to attend the open house. The kaizen was put in place, and the response was very positive. 40% of the trades sent in their bids based on the specification package emailed to them. This saved time for the tradespeople, but it also gave Habitat Kent early visibility to which parts of the house had enough bids and which elements needed additional attention.

With the future state in place, more partners bidding on the projects will ensure that Habitat Kent has an ample supply of trades to meet its ever-growing list of housing projects. Habitat Kent is not stopping there. It had been manually printing and filing all bids. However, with the exception of some bids from government funding, most bids could be handled and stored electronically. It plans to include the ability to have the trades electronically sign the bid projects, thus eliminating the wastes of printing, signing, scanning, and emailing the bids back to the Habitat Kent office.

The Habitat Kent staff has adopted a continuous improvement mentality, and after implementing the future state, it is making a series of other improvements in their operations.

SUMMARY

The One Main Thing – Use value stream mapping to innovate and transform the work in the office.

STUDY QUESTIONS

1. Why is mapping of office value streams so important in making transformations?
2. What are the three reasons for value stream mapping?
3. Who is the focus of the value stream map?
4. What moves through the map?
5. What are the typical improvement goals for value stream mapping transformations?
6. What is the formula (or steps) in the value stream mapping method?
7. How can sticky notes be used to speed up the value stream mapping method?
8. What are the definitions of processing time, cycle time, wait time, and percentage complete and accurate?
9. What are the useful techniques and questions to ask in moving from current state to future state?

7

Post-Value Stream Mapping Workshop Activities

MAKING THE KAIZENS VISIBLE TO SUSTAIN MOMENTUM

One litmus test of a successful workshop is that the team feels ownership of the outcome of the workshop and the future state design. A goal of the workshop is to have an empowered team willing to take charge of its own value stream and initiate the improvements to make the work easier with better quality results. The challenge is to capture the excitement and euphoria of the workshop and convert it into action in the days and weeks following the workshop. The kaizen worksheet, as represented in Table 6.2, can be used to convert the workshop kaizens into an action plan. When the team generates the action plan in the workshop and immediately begins work on the kaizens, the momentum can be maintained.

The last day of the workshop is spent creating the detail kaizen plans on the A3 format. This creates a detailed action plan for all actions coming out of the workshop. The A3 sheets also become the reporting mechanism for the workshop. The A3 is the main communication vehicle for the kaizen efforts during the 90-day implementation phase.

Why use an A3 versus PowerPoint or some other communication vehicle?

A metric A3 size format (or 11" x 17" size paper) has become the universal Lean communication vehicle; it works equally well in manufacturing and in the office.

Why use an A3?

- It is easy to read.
- It provides a simple and elegant summary of the key project tasks.

- It is concise and to the point.
- It supports the visual display of information.

The last point is key. The A3 should become a visual part of the project. It should be used to create a visual project wall. A visual project wall consists of the value stream map and the A3s the team is using to track the kaizen efforts. The visual wall provides instant feedback on the status of the improvement efforts. Over the 90 days of implementation, the visual project wall becomes "command central" for the value stream transformation activities. The weekly project team meeting should be held at the wall where the A3s are displayed. The report-outs to the leadership team can happen at the same location using the A3s.

By displaying the A3s in a public area, the whole company becomes aware of the transformational improvements taking place. These should not be hidden or only pulled out for the update meetings. The goal with these A3s, as with all Lean visuals, is visual persistence. Since they are displayed, they may show "red status" if a task or an entire A3 falls behind; they become another opportunity to communicate the "culture of red." The fact that a project element turns red is not something for the team to dread reporting or to worry that management will punish them for being late. Instead, red on a project should be recognized as a realistic status update. Figure 7.1 shows the schedule portion of an A3 project plan with several items turned red. In this case, the team would be reporting out for the week of 2/13. A red item needs to be reported along with the countermeasures the team is taking to turn the red back to green. Leadership will need to applaud the team for showing red status and remind the team members that, "In a Lean culture, a red status is perfectly fine as long as the team is addressing the underlying root cause that is causing the problem." Red on a project plan gives the team the opportunity to discuss with the leadership where help might be needed.

KAIZEN PLANS OR LARGER PROJECTS

In many cases, a larger project with multiple kaizens will be broken down into individual A3s. In these cases, the master A3 keeps track of the overall progress as shown in Figure 7.2, but there is additional

Implementation Plan Example

Standard use of A3 Implementation Plan including use of comment field and responsible group (notice that each item stands on its own)

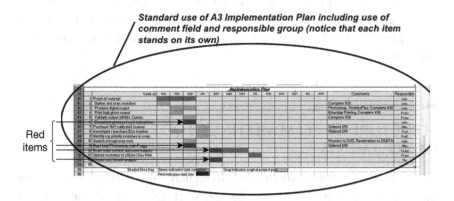

Red items

FIGURE 7.1
A detailed A3 implementation plan with red and green status.

Implementation Plan Example (Larger Project)

Each item on the plan has it's own separate detailed AE (separate A3's not shown here)

	Week of	10/14	10/21	10/28	11/4	11/11	11/18	11/25	12/2	12/9	12/16	12/23	12/30	1/6	Comments	Responsible
1	Comprehenisve List for culling														As complete as possible	Dan
2	Process for potential culling - for mfg														Waiting on a critical resource	Ron
3	Enhance existing decision sheet														Complete	Dave
4	Define approval steps for late adds														Complete	Sheryl
5	Culling data document is sortable															Sheryl
6	Streamline the printed list process														Complete	Cindy
7	Training for complete process														Can not start until all other objectives complete	Dan
8	Create Mfg database process														Training in January	Kathi

FIGURE 7.2
A high-level plan for kaizens.

detail in the next level of kaizens, each maintained on its own A3 document. As the Lean initiative ramps up, multiple parallel improvements happen across the entire organization. These parallel efforts can be tracked on a master A3 visual project wall. On this wall, high-level A3s track the various projects occurring across the organization.

STRUCTURE OF TEAM MEETINGS TO TRACK IMPROVEMENTS

As the team members return to their regular jobs after a value stream mapping workshop, they have the tendency to focus on the work at their desks and the daily fires that need to be put out. To keep the momentum going, the kaizen owners meet weekly to give updates on the progress made. Update meetings using the A3 should be brief and to the point. They need not take more than 30 minutes. The A3 plan is the only document used, and PowerPoint is avoided, which ensures that the updates for each kaizen are short, accurate, and current. Each kaizen owner gives an update on progress made in his or her respected area of responsibility using the A3: a quick review of completed items and then a focus on any lagging red items and help that may be needed.

The project manager provides an important role in keeping the team together during the implementation. The project manager attends the workshop and carries the plan to completion. Table 7.1 shows all of the activities of the project manager during and after the workshop.

GETTING THE LEADERS INVOLVED IMPROVES TEAM ACCOUNTABILITY

To keep the team on track, and to keep the leadership team informed, regular reviews are scheduled. After the workshop, the leadership team joins the team every 30 days during the team's regular A3 project review meeting. The leadership team is kept aware of the progress. If the team is facing difficulty moving forward, the leaders have a chance to hear about it and remove any road blocks or barriers. The 30-day reviews are like a secret sauce to ensure that the kaizen efforts are going forward

TABLE 7.1

Typical Workshop Schedule

Activity	Who Attends	Frequency and Duration
Workshop current state – day 1	Workshop team, Lean facilitator, **project manager**	One day
Workshop future state – day 2	Workshop team, Lean facilitator, **project manager**, leadership panel at the end of the day	One day Leaders attend for 1 hour
Workshop planning, A3 plans created – day 3	Workshop team, Lean facilitator, **project manager**, leadership panel at the end of the day	One day Leaders attend for 1 hour
Weekly kaizen A3 plan review	Kaizen owners, Lean facilitator (optional), **project manager**	Weekly over the next 90 days – 30 minutes (total of 13 meetings)
30-, 60-, and 90-day leadership review of A3 plans	Leadership panel, kaizen owners, Lean facilitator, and **project manager**	Monthly over the next 90 days – 30 minutes (total of 3 meetings)

and keeping everything on pace. This disciplined approach helps to fight against the tendency for the efforts to delay or get buried underneath other corporate initiatives.

MINI CASE STUDY – A MODEL PLAN FOR THE TRANSFORMATION OF A VALUE STREAM

A team at a Midwest company, located in Denver, held a workshop to value stream map their development system. A dozen or so members of their new product development group met for a 3-day value stream mapping workshop. They did the current state map on day 1, the future state on day 2, and implementation plans on day 3. The A3 kaizen plans were drafted on the third day of the workshop. In this case, the team selected 5 key kaizens for implementation in the first 90 days. The Lean facilitator insisted that the A3 kaizen plans were well laid out and detailed before the teams left on the third day. The A3 plans were shared with the leadership team at the end of the third day by the kaizen owners. The leadership team suggested some adjustments to the plans, and they were made to the plans before everyone left for the day.

Staying on track with the improvement plans is difficult for busy office workers, and it was no different at this company. Once the workshop participants returned to their "regular jobs" after the workshop, they had a backlog of email, many pressures, deliverables, and deadlines. Even though they left the workshop enthusiastic and excited to achieve the future state, improving the work might have slipped to the background. Adam was the project manager appointed during scoping. He attended all 3 days of the workshop. It was his role to keep the kaizen plans moving forward. The Lean facilitator encouraged Adam to schedule and lead the weekly kaizen owner reviews and to let the leadership know if other corporate priorities began to hinder progress on the kaizens. After the workshop, Adam scheduled the leadership panel reviews for dates that were 30, 60, and 90 days from the workshop. This locked in these milestone dates on everyone's calendars. Adam also scheduled the weekly review of the A3 kaizen plans with the kaizen owners and led the meetings.

At the weekly kaizen reviews, the teams discussed progress of the efforts and adjusted the plans with additional details. At the first 30-day review, the teams showed their A3 plans to the leadership panel. The A3s plans they brought were quite detailed, and they displayed "red" status where needed to show the tasks that were getting behind. The leadership team reacted positively, and without alarm, to the red items and looked for ways to help the team move forward. This disciplined approach kept the plans on track.

MEASURING AND TRACKING THE BENEFITS OF THE WORKSHOP

Key metrics like reduction in total cycle time, number of process steps, and rework percentage are shown on the project plan A3 and updated on a 30-day interval. The measures appear at the bottom of the A3 template. This is designed to show regular progress for both the team and the leadership. Figure 7.3 gives an example of the measures shown in the lower right-hand corner of an A3. In this case the update is

	Measure	Baseline	90 d Target	30 d check	60 d check	90 d check 11/13	Reasons for not hitting your target measure and comments
						Outcome Measures	
1	Visual Board with weekly Stand-up meeting	None exists	Exists	In place		Using Regularly	Using feedback survey after 1st week. NO etc
2	Rework after reaching HR office	Greater than 50%	90% correct			not measured, bu	Since Tuesday meeting review. - significantly improved. Timing issues .. late notice. Using the start date, and access can be done early. Preventing IT hold-ups.
3	New staff/faculty/adjunct info entered early	Loaded after 8/15	@ appointment				Only one situation. Lack of paper work from person - Paid 9/15 not 9/1. (Not HR caused).
4	Rework of IT, Salary, or other Colleague data	Greater than 50%	Less than 10%				A few part-time faculty did not bring in paperwork. Etty now cross training to enter this information. Per Lisa, LDAP information is coming faster with assigned department and means they can access systems when they come in.
5	60 step process reduced to 30 steps	60 steps	30 steps				

FIGURE 7.3

A3 measures.

occurring at 60 days. The team has completed 4 of the 5 workshop metrics, with only number 2 outstanding.

CASE STUDY – RAPID VALUE STREAM TRANSFORMATION AT A COLLEGE

Calvin College was the subject of a case study in an earlier chapter and discussed how they organized for a Lean cultural transformation. Calvin embarked on a number of early value stream mapping exercises. It had some experience in what a transformational value stream workshop was all about. In the 2015/2016 school year, the federal government had made a change to the rules of filing for student aid. The changes allowed parents to use their prior year tax returns for filing. Up to this point, parents of prospective students needed to rush to fill out their tax return in January to start the financial aid application process for the fall semester. With the changes, the parents could use the prior year tax return and colleges and universities could begin accepting financial aid applications much earlier. Calvin wanted to make it easier for parents to apply and to show prospective students what financial aid they would receive from the college.

In order to make the changes, a major overhaul of the value stream would be required. The college ran a value stream mapping workshop in the winter of 2016 to understand the current work method and make plans to adjust the plans for a future state. The project started out with a scoping session and then followed the workshop methodology outlined in this chapter. The homework phase included a Gemba walk of the value stream and one-on-one interviews with everyone. As one might imagine, the work was complex. The current state showed all of the things that would need to be adjusted. The future state map helped the team outline the changes that needed to be made. There were well over 20 kaizens. The changes to the value stream were extensive and included the following:

- Decisions that needed to be made earlier
- Earlier information to counselors
- Changes in information packages that went out to students
- Earlier filing and deadline dates to communicate to students and parents
- System changes in the college's computing platform
- Changed dates for scholarship and grant decisions
- Moving dates for notification of awards

The college used the value stream mapping method to transform their financial aid process and outline all of the changes that would be required. Figure 7.4 shows one section of the larger future state map. Here the reader can see the intent to inform the students of their financial aid awards, and several of the kaizens that need to occur in order to make it possible.

The kaizens were listed in a kaizen plan, and each of the most complex had a project plan A3 filled out and posted on the wall showing the value stream. One master A3 90-day plan was used to show all of the kaizens that needed to be done to complete the overall project. The team used the master A3 as a status update on the transformational value stream project. This was a rapid timeline, but it was required to make all of the changes in time to prepare for the financial aid application timeline for the next school year, which would shift forward dramatically to allow for earlier applications, financial aid awards, and admissions to the college.

The kaizen leaders adopted a weekly cadence of report-outs of the status of the A3 plans. The plans were also shared with the Lean leaders on a regular basis. The college's Lean coach guided them through the kaizen reporting process and practice of frequent stand-up meetings to report on progress. The regular report-outs kept the kaizens on track.

Not all of the kaizens were green for the entire project. This was a culture shift for the team. The idea that red was okay to display in

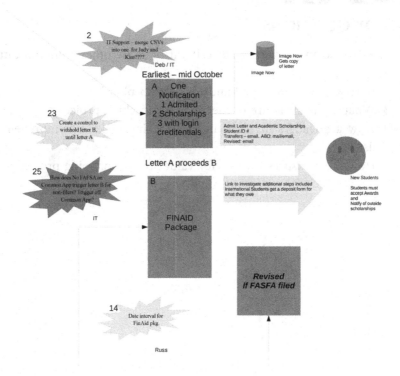

FIGURE 7.4
Sample of a future state high-level map with kaizens.

an area where people would see the status took some getting used to by the leaders. They came from a philosophy of not calling attention to red. However, in a Lean culture, red can be displayed in a visible place.

The PPY financial aid workshop became a differentiator for the college compared to other comparable colleges in the Midwest.

SUMMARY

The One Main Thing – regular weekly check-ins with the team and 30-day check-ins with the leadership team keep the kaizen efforts moving.

STUDY QUESTIONS

1. Why use an A3 versus PowerPoint or some other communication vehicle?
2. How are large projects handled with A3 plans?
3. What is the structure of meetings for tracking projects?
4. How are leaders involved in the tracking of kaizen improvement lists?
5. How are measures tracked for value stream mapping projects?

Section III

Building Lean into the Culture of the Team

8

Education – Learning and Practicing

TRANSFORMING THE CULTURE ONE LEAN VERB AT A TIME

In a Lean culture, everyone from the leadership to the employees knows and applies the Lean concepts. There cannot be only learning and knowing because if you only learn about Lean, then Lean is just a noun. The knowing about Lean must be accompanied by *doing* Lean. *Lean is not a noun; Lean is a verb.* Lean is something that the organization does. To this end, all training of Lean ideas and concepts needs to be followed up with doing. In class, exercises, and then immediate application to a problem area after the class are critical. Applying Lean immediately after learning about Lean helps to make Lean a verb within the organization. Why is this important? In a Lean company, employees are doing Lean as part of their daily jobs. Everyone needs to be involved in solving problems and making improvements. All members of the staff are submitting ideas on how to get better. The leaders are demonstrating Lean by working on systematic problems, and the staff is working at problems at the team level. Some people have asked me if you will run out of problems. My answer is, "Don't worry, you will never run out of problems to solve. Every process is full of wastes and various issues, and all of them need to be fixed or improved." Every value stream has handoffs, delays, and inefficiencies. These value stream issues are the constant targets for the organization. The organization needs to train people how to see the wastes, and how to remove and prevent the wastes that enter work.

If Lean is to become part of the culture, the principles and their application must be well understood. New behaviors and practices can be infused into the culture when everyone in the culture is working toward the same goals and speaking the same language. Speaking the same language means taking away the mystery of some of the Lean lingo. If you introduce Lean words, especially in the Japanese original, then they have to be de-mystified. I try to only use the words in Japanese that are universally used. Common Japanese Lean words such as kaizen, Gemba, heijunka, and poka-yoke are defined for the organization. Less common Lean words are better left for use by the Lean sensei and kept out of the vocabulary of the organization. The English versions are just as important: improvement event, go and see, pull system, and error-proofing. Translating the words is one level but teaching the employees how to do these things is the goal. The Lean vocabulary must become the verbs and a call to action. Table 8.1 gives some typical Lean words the organization should become familiar with since they are frequently used to describe Lean activities.

Nothing is more powerful or more important to driving a Lean culture in the office than initial and ongoing education around the Lean behavior.

TABLE 8.1

Common Lean Words for Office Lean

Common Lean Words	Translated into Verbs and Action
Kaizen	Continually improving the process
Gemba or Gemba-gembutsu	Going to the place to see the wastes and understand the process; this is done by leaders and staff.
Value stream	Walking the process, step by step, and seeing the work
Flow	Eliminating interruptions to the flow of information
Heijunka	A pull scheduling system that signals the supplying process to send output
Poka-yoke	Building in waste prevention so that process problems don't re-occur
Problem solving	Completing root cause problem solving on any critical problems or process interruptions
Visual boards	Using visual boards to show the process and display the health of the process
Obeya room	Translated as "big room" or any large project room or wall used for Lean visuals

Overview training that teaches awareness of the Lean methods is an excellent way to launch the program. As teams start to apply the concepts in their areas, just-in-time training and coaching are great methods for immediately applying the concepts to the problems. Then ongoing training is key to educating new members of leadership and the staff.

NEVER STOP TEACHING LEAN

Since Lean is a journey, and a way of life, the training must be continued as the organization changes and new staff and leaders are brought on board. Lean concepts are easy, but there is a tendency for practices and habits to decay over time. Teaching Lean and keeping it fresh are key to helping to ensure that the practices continue in the organization. Here are some reasons to never stop teaching Lean.

- New employees and staff
- Existing employees who need or would like a refresher
- Cross-learning in the organization
- Some departments still need to learn Lean
- The Lean vocabulary is not part of the language in all parts of the organization.

THE LEAN TRAINING MODEL INVOLVES PRACTICING LEAN

Since the goal of Lean is to get the involvement of everyone in the organization, the training model also needs to focus on action. This makes Lean training different from other types of "class room" training. Most organizations share information in the education and on-boarding process. There is a lot to share about office policies, standards, and procedures when new employees come on board. Much of that training is done online. Lean training is different because it is hands on. Every concept or principle taught is followed by an exercise and an application of the concepts. Table 8.2 is a listing of the recommended topics for training in office Lean. The goal in each module of the training is the immediate application of the concepts when the attendees get back to their area.

TABLE 8.2

Lean Basics are Followed by Immediate Application.

Lean Basics	Immediate Application
Eliminate wastes	Identify wastes in the office process and suggest ways to eliminate them.
Improve flow	Look for processes that do not flow and work is pushed (e.g., email) and install processes to pull the work.
Eliminate the root cause	Select a problem in your area and apply the PDCA (plan-do-check-act) or problem-solving methodology to fix the problem.
Value stream mapping	Map a cross-functional process with symbols and use the map to identify the improvements needed.
Go and see	Follow a process from person to person and look for the inefficiencies and wastes.
One-page A3s	Create an improvement A3 project plan for a project.
Visual boards	Build a visual board of a process to be used by the team to track the work.
Continuous improvement	Create a simple team idea board and ask team members to start submitting and implementing process improvements.

In the Lean training modules, every concept and principle is followed by a hands-on exercise to apply the concepts, so the participants get a flavor for how to apply the concepts. Lean is not just for the experts and the black belts in the organization. The goal is to put the tools in everyone's hands.

HELPING THE ORGANIZATION DISCOVER WHAT IT NEEDS TO KNOW ABOUT LEAN

The organization needs to understand the basics of the Lean approach. What follows are the topics and practices universal to the Lean methods.

The Definition of Value

Value is always defined from the customer at the end of the value stream. In an office, the customer receives the product or service the organization offers. Each person in the value stream needs to understand who the customer is and what is needed from the process.

Common exercises involve asking people to list the steps in the value stream of which they are part, who the customer is, and what role they play in the value stream.

Eliminate the Wastes from the Process

Chapter 2 defined the wastes in some detail. The education around wastes is to communicate the wastes that are commonly found in office and administrative process. The challenge and the goal are to know the waste definition and then have everyone in the organization begin identifying the wastes. A useful exercise is to have each student list a waste in his or her experience and to think of ways to eliminate it.

Finding the Root of the Problem

Problems have many causes, and people often have misleading ideas on what will permanently remove the problem. Office culture often lives by a break-and-fix methodology, which must be broken. The tendency is to identify a quick solution for problems and move on. Often, however, the solution is temporary, and the problem re-occurs. The situation is forgotten, and when the problem resurfaces, another temporary solution is put in place. This method of placing Band Aids and temporary counter measures on office problems leads to complex processes with far too many validation steps.

The goal is to get the Lean students to recognize how to move beyond the break-and-fix mentality to do some break-and-fix analysis. A useful exercise is to have the students look for a problem that requires some root-cause thinking, identify the problem and the root cause, and then propose the solution. Table 8.3 gives a list of thought starters on where to look for problems in office value streams. There is always a rich field of problems inside of the office processes for problem solving.

THE LEAN TRAINING MODEL

Since office workers are stretched thin and have difficulty leaving their jobs for extended periods, the best approach is to break the training

TABLE 8.3

Where to Look for Problems

- Production issues caused by office errors
- Customer interruptions and delays
- Office processes where work doesn't but could flow
- Points at which inventory and backlogs build up in the process
- Re-occurring or repeating problems
- Quality problems in data or information
- Critical incidences in the IT systems
- Tasks that generate rework
- Things that increase cycle time
- Situations where documentation does not exist or is not followed

---

concepts into learning modules and schedule them over several weeks. In this way, a module or two can be completed each week, and more importantly, homework and hands-on activities can be assigned between the classes. Additionally, certain learning modules can be used to do just-in-time training for teams who are going to implement Lean activities such as value stream mapping, root-cause problem solving, team idea boards, etc. Figure 8.1 lists the recommend training to be offered to office works who are new to Lean.

From experience, organizing training in modules and delivering them to teams across multiple weeks or just in time is the best way to organize internal training. However, if an external Lean coach or consultant is delivering the training, this timing becomes more difficult. An effective alternative model when using external consultants is to appoint internal coaches and/or leaders who can learn and teach the materials. This train-the-trainer approach is effective, and then the organization can rely on the internal leaders and coaches to deliver the modules in the future to a model that fits the organization.

There are several benefits to having internal training. The materials can be customized and adapted to the organization's methods and language. The material can also be tied to the corporate strategy and initiatives. At one company in the heartland of America, the leadership had developed a Lean strategy called "High Speed, Low Drag." The internal Lean team adapted the learning exercises and activities to demonstrate ways to increase speed (a.k.a. value stream flow) and

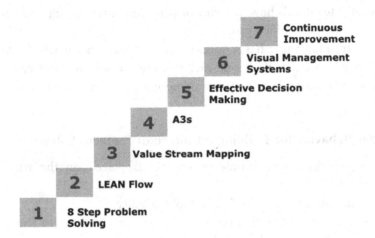

FIGURE 8.1
Typical Lean learning modules. These are separated for delivering training just in time or spreading out the delivery across several days and weeks.

reduce the drag (a.k.a. wastes) in the office processes. The students in the class easily identified areas where speed in the office needed to increase, and there was no shortage of examples of drag on the office processes.

A key philosophy in Lean is that everyone does Lean. In fact, the employees and staff in the organization will not keep doing Lean unless they see the leaders doing Lean. Training for leaders is critical for the Lean program if the leaders are also going to practice Lean. Leaders will need to work on their own problems, and they will need to support the Lean work done by the teams.

BUILDING A LEAN CULTURE BY HAVING LEADERS TRAIN

The topics and tools are the same for leadership training in the office as what the rest of the organization is taught. While the Lean basics are the same, most of the focus for leadership is on the behaviors needed to build a Lean culture.

For instance, to build a culture of problem solvers, the leadership team needs to build a safe environment for raising problems. The leadership team will have a series of activities surrounding each of the topics in the Lean office program.

Each training topic has a specific set of behaviors on which leaders need to be coached. Each one makes a great discussion exercise, with the leaders offering how they can demonstrate the new practices.

Leader Behavior for Building a Culture of Problem Solvers

- When discussing problems – focus is placed on the why, not the who
- Allow problems to surface without penalty
- Create an environment where people can continue to learn and grow through problem solving
- Encourage members to take risks then use mistakes as learning opportunities
- Identify situations that require the use of the problem-solving method
- Discuss lessons learned from difficult situations
- Recognize individual and team efforts in problem solving
- Hold ourselves accountable for problem solving everyday
- Share Lean success stories.

Leader Behavior for Building Flow into Process

- Be able to identify processes that push information (e.g., all processes that operate only via email are push).
- Support value stream mapping to examine and improve flow
- Be willing to stop and fix processes that are not flowing
- Walk the process (Gemba) to determine flow

Leadership Behavior for Looking at Value Streams

- Ask for value stream maps for key office processes.
- Be a vision setter for how a process should work.
- Set high goals for the teams working on value streams.
- Schedule time for workshops and free up people.
- Ask for A3 improvement plans.
- Attend team meetings regularly for status updates.

Leaders Behavior Surrounding Visuals

- Learning to recognize process health
- Building visuals that show the current process health (not backward measurements)
- Looking for involvement of everyone on the team in making improvements
- The various types of visuals and their purposes – project tracking, progression of work, resource balancing, process throughput, etc.
- Participating in stand-up meetings, while letting the team run and take responsibility for meeting

CASE STUDY – A TEAM IMPROVEMENT BOARD GETS A BOOST AFTER A TRAINING EVENT

During a training class, the department admin, Cheryl, came to the class introducing Lean concepts. Since every module contained education material followed by an exercise, she worked through each exercise. After the first module, she went back and identified the various wastes in the office processes. After the second module, she looked at the upstream and downstream people in the value stream. She Gemba walked the process following a tracking form she used and talked to the people who supply information to her and to the people to whom she handed off information. She was recognizing the wastes in the process and starting to get ideas around what improvements might be made. After the module on visuals and stand-up meetings, the class was encouraged to build their own simple improvement board to capture ideas from the team. She found an open white board in the office and created the first improvement board for her department. It was nothing elaborate, and the lines were simply drawn on the board. Beautifying the board would come later after the team started to build up their Lean skillsets and determined exactly how they wanted to use the board. Besides building the board, she and the team decided to hold stand-up meetings. The team had tried stand-up meetings once before, but there had been no structure to them. As is typical with initial attempts, the stand-up meetings in the past went long, people did

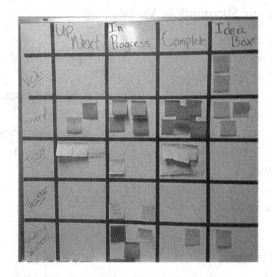

FIGURE 8.2
A simple Lean improved board after the training class.

not actually stand, and after a while they were abandoned. With the information she learned in the class, they held a stand-up meeting with a standard agenda and kept the meetings to under 15 minutes. Cheryl learned that *the primary purpose of the boards is to use them as a place to log improvements to the process*. She was able to populate the board with many of the improvement ideas that she discovered while looking for wastes in the process. Figure 8.2 shows the improvement board, and Cheryl has many of the action items (sticky notes) for improvements. Therefore, it was no surprise that most of the sticky notes on the board were written by her, and a number of them were assigned to her as well.

SUMMARY

The One Main Thing – Effective training is applied immediately toward process improvements.

STUDY QUESTIONS

1. Why is it important to apply Lean immediately after learning Lean?
2. What Japanese Lean words are commonly used?
3. Why is an ongoing Lean education effort important to the organization?
4. What are some leader behaviors for building a problem-solving culture?

9

Office Visuals and Space

THE PURPOSE OF VISUALS IN THE OFFICE

Visuals in the office were initially a foreign idea, and not every office facilities manager is in favor of interrupting the office landscape with visuals. However, with so much information typically buried in reports, PowerPoints, and other electronic systems, visual boards help to make the health of the office value streams visible. In Lean, visual display of information is intended to make the value stream visible so that it becomes the focus of daily team stand-up meetings centered on improving the work. The ultimate goal is to have visuals in the office do the same things they do on the manufacturing floor; namely, make the process health visible and drive improvements of the value stream. For this reason, team spaces with visual white boards should be utilized and frequently (daily) updated to check on the process.

When thinking about what to display in a team area, the focus is to be on the indicators of process health. The contents of the visual boards are the metrics of process health. Typical visual display content includes the follow:

- Key wastes to monitor or watch
- Critical points in the process where there is "risk" of errors being made
- Processes steps where the pace of work is critical to the customer
- Milestone activities performed within the value stream to ensure that the team achieves the desired result
- Quality metrics through the process or at the end of the process
- Flow interrupters captured with corrective actions

- Leading metrics that point to the health of the process
- Anything that is valuable for management to review on Gemba walks

VISUAL ENVIRONMENTS

Space needs to accommodate Lean visuals. In many offices, there is no common shared space in which visuals can be displayed. Initially, any vertical surface might provide the space for visuals. This might be done in a hallway or on a conference room wall. Ideally, the visuals should be located near the team space or in a space the team regularly visits. Eventually, the visual boards should be integrated into the office landscape and be part of the location of daily stand-up meetings. Good visual spaces have an abundance of whiteboard space and an appropriate blend of analog (paper display) and integrated digital monitors. Figure 9.1 shows how visual displays include both digital monitors and analog (paper) displayed side-by-side The analog information is used for the display of metrics, kaizen plans, root-cause problem solving, and department initiatives that do not change rapidly. Digital monitors display real-time value stream data that change rapidly yet must be monitored in real time. Team stand-up meetings occur in these settings.

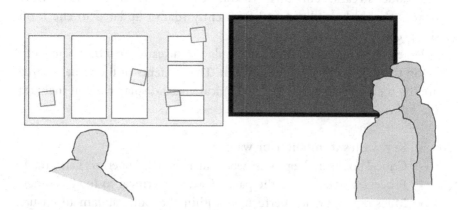

FIGURE 9.1

Lean visual spaces blend analog (paper) displays with electronic monitors for electronic real-time information.

VISUALS FOR TRACKING PROCESS FLOW

When the value stream crosses multiple boundaries, visuals display process steps across the functions. Teams use physical boards to show the progression of work through the value stream. When the process steps are made visual, bottlenecks and frequent process interrupts become visible as well. These then become the focus of process improvements and corrective action activities. An effective visual in the office will drive pull across the office value stream. In manufacturing, there is a focus on one-piece flow and pull systems. Likewise, the pull systems in the office center around the visual boards put in place to drive the process.

A typical tracking wall (see Figure 9.2) shows project names in the rows and steps in the columns. The visuals quickly show the progress of the projects through the steps. The columns represent the steps in the process. The pace (or duration) is labeled at the top of each column as either .5 or 1 day. The squares on the visual board are split diagonally to show the target date vs. the actual date. The red/green status of each step is clearly visible on the visual board. The visual board keeps the team informed of the status

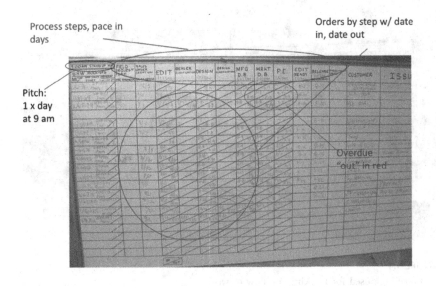

FIGURE 9.2

The visuals show projects moving through the value stream.

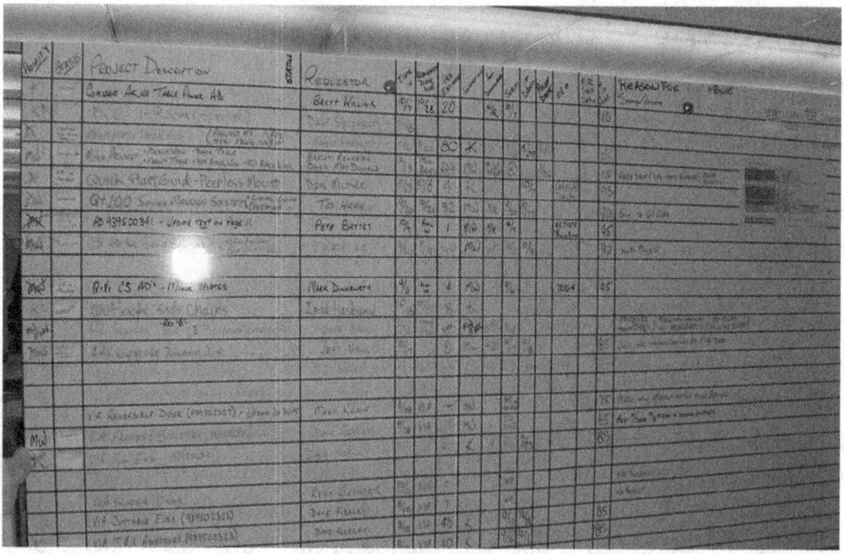

FIGURE 9.3
A typical office visual comparing projects and their status.

FIGURE 9.4
An office area used for tracking the flow of work.

of the work moving through their value stream. The frequency of the team meetings is once per day at 9:00 am.

In Figure 9.3, the dates are recorded for when projects were received by the team and when they are due to be finished. The leftmost column indicates priority, and the sticky notes give instant feedback on the status of the work.

In the visual example shown in Figure 9.4, the folders on the vertical wall show the steps in the process. In this case, the work is actually placed in the folders. Each column of folders represents a step in the office value stream. Even though the work is done in the computers at the workers' desks, the current location of each piece of work in the value stream can be seen. Out cards are used to indicate that a piece of work is back on someone's desk. Each person works on only one item at a time. This functional group moves thousands of pages of documentation through these steps every two months.

TIER I VISUAL BOARD AND MEETING

A critical activity in managing a value stream for process health involves the concept of tiered accountability from the team. The team monitors the process, and each level of management is linked into the discussion. Figure 9.4 is one example of a Tier I visual. The universal rule of the tiered visuals and metrics is that they should reflect the current status of the work. That is to say, they should never display metrics about what happened last month or even last week. In a Lean system, the visuals provide an instantaneous snapshot of the current health of the value stream. The team visual boards should consist of the following:

- Key strategies and focus areas for improvement
- Leading indicators and metrics of process health across the value stream
- The work for the day and the deadlines for the work
- Problems and issues that have appeared and need action
- Active Lean improvement projects against problems and issues

The best strategy is to start small and create visual boards within one process area. The visuals start with the teams closest to the work. They are always the first to know of any issues or changes in the incoming work that has to be done. Eventually, multiple teams and departments will create their own visual boards.

The team's daily stand-up meetings always follow a standard agenda. A team leader may lead the discussion; however, each team member should be expected to run a team meeting. The team will meet at least daily at the visual tracking system, and depending on the speed of the work, they many even meet twice per day. The meeting is attended by the knowledgeable workers in the process and their supervisor. The supervisor will cascade upward any key information that needs to be acted on at the next level of leadership.

Tier I Meeting
Who attends the Tier I meeting? Team and supervisor (or team leader)
Purpose: Discuss current work within the team
Status questions covered in the meeting:

- What work is in the backlog?
- What is the status of the work and priorities?
- Exception handling of unusual or "hot" requests?
- What are the coverage needs?
- Are there issues and problems to work through?
- What improvement ideas are being worked on at the team level?

The desired outcome of the tier 1 team meeting is to assess the current status of the work, understand issues, assign action items, and highlight areas for future problem solving or improvement activities.

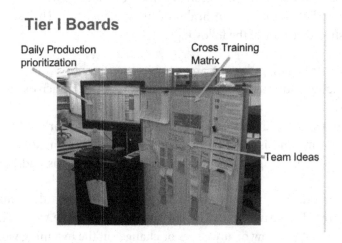

FIGURE 9.5
A typical Tier I team board within a team area.

TABLE 9.1

Typical Tier I Board Content

Description	Purpose
List of incoming work	Keeping the backlog of work in view and assigning individuals to the work
Vacation/staffing schedule	Understand who is available for the work
Cross-training matrix	Understand who is expert, proficient, or beginner in each job function, with a plan for training
Standard meeting agenda	Detailed stand-up meeting agenda to ensure the meeting runs smoothly and quickly and to allow any team member to run the meeting; stand-up meetings are held to 15 minutes.
Team idea system	Ideas at the team level go through the 4 steps: Capture To-do (prioritized to work on next) Doing (team is working on this) Done

Figure 9.5 shows an example of a Tier I visual board. Ideally, Tier I visual boards are as close to the team area as possible, where the team meeting happens on a daily basis. This team is managing a complex influx of orders. They self-manage who works on what. They are focused on throughput and quality. The team depth is being increased through cross-training on all of the various functions that the team must perform. They are trying to ensure that they are relying on internal experts. All knowledge is shared across the work team, and ideally anyone can do any job. The team also has its own idea system. Table 9.1 gives the typical content covered at a Tier I meeting.

TIER II VISUAL BOARD AND MEETING

The next level of boards is for the next level in the organization. This level also has a need to keep a pulse on the process on a daily basis. They too are watching out for process problems across the value stream. However, their focus is one level higher at the cross-functional teams that are in the process.

Tier II Meeting

Who attends the Tier II meeting? Supervisors (or team leaders) and manager

Purpose: Discuss current work across the teams

Status questions to be covered in the meeting:

- What work is in the backlog?
- What is the current status and the work priorities?
- What are the cross-team issues and opportunities?
- How is the work balanced across the team?
- What issues and problems should be and are being worked on?
- What are the improvement updates at the supervisor level?
- What are the cross-training needs?
- Are there opportunities to adjust the team balance?

Figure 9.6 gives an example of a typical Tier II visual board. The Tier II visual board should be as close to the team area as possible, near where the team meets on a daily basis. The supervisors and manager also review the status of work (just as the team reviews the work), but with a focus on what is happening between the teams.

The supervisors and the manager are looking at team balance and work coverage. They are concerned with team depth and opportunities for cross-training to spread the knowledge across the team. The supervisors

Tier II Boards

FIGURE 9.6

A typical Tier II board at the supervisor/manager level.

TABLE 9.2

Typical Tier II Board Content

Description	Purpose
List of current issues	With the knowledge of the backlog, the supervisors can bring forward problems and issues in the process.
Staffing schedule	Discuss cross-training needs and potential rebalancing of team members to handle shifting incoming work.
Key leading process metrics	A process metric that the supervisors are tracking and watching; multiple metrics can be tracked
Standard meeting agenda	Detailed stand-up meeting agenda to ensure the meeting runs smoothly and quickly and to allow any team member to run the meeting; Tier II standup meetings are held at 15 minutes.
Improvement ideas	Ideas that are owned by the supervisors (or team leaders) that stretch across the teams.
Root-cause problem solving	Critical issues, problem solving, and root causes/corrective actions are tracked at the supervisor level.

have their own problems and ideas to work on. Table 9.2 gives the typical content covered at a Tier II meeting.

TIER III VISUAL BOARD AND MEETING

The supervisor will cascade upward any key information that needs to be acted on at the next level of leadership at the Tier III meetings. These meetings are held daily or at least multiple times per week. The desired outcome of the Tier III managers meeting is to assess trends of the work and to understand issues across the value stream that should be assigned at the management level. Action items and improvement activities are assigned to the various functional managers and tracked. Strategic initiatives and improvements are discussed for improving the overall values stream with a focus across the various functions in the process.

Tier III Meeting
Who attends the Tier III Meeting? Managers with the Director or VP
Purpose: Discuss direction of key process metrics and discuss projects and corrective action to make across the value stream

Status questions to be covered in the Tier III meeting:

- What are the trends in value stream metrics?
- If the trend is red, what is the corrective action?
- What are the incoming and future demands on the process?
- How should we adjust or balance staffing levels?
- What key process problems are the teams currently working on?
- What strategic process improvements are being made by the managers?
- What is the level of engagement in improvement efforts by the teams?

Figure 9.7 depicts the visuals at the Tier III level.

The visuals should be in an open area that the both the leaders and the team have regular access to and will see frequently. The managers, director, and other leaders will review the current trends in the work and look at key leading process metrics. The opportunity to improve the value stream is discussed, and improvement projects are displayed. The managers own and track their own improvement projects. Table 9.3 lists the typical content covered at a Tier III meeting.

Leadership meetings at the Tier III boards can be difficult to time-box into 15 minutes. These meetings can be split into smaller meetings with

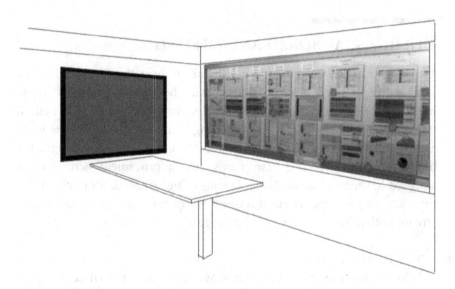

FIGURE 9.7
A typical Tier III board at the manager/director level.

TABLE 9.3

Typical Tier III Board Content

Description	Purpose
Key strategies and initiatives	Link the organization strategy to the initiatives in each department
Current trend metrics	Understand the critical process metrics (there could be multiple tracked) and determine their direction (red/green)
Pareto charts and process analysis	Each functional area displays detail analysis behind the trend metrics.
Improvement ideas	Ideas that are owned by the managers that stretch across the functions
Value stream improvement	Review projects between the function to improve the value stream (displayed electronically on monitor)
Root-cause problem solving	Critical issues, problem solving, and root causes/corrective actions are tracked at the manager level (displayed electronically on monitor).
Standard meeting agenda	Detailed stand-up meeting agenda to ensure the meeting runs smoothly and quickly and to allow any team member to run the meeting. Manager stand-ups are held to 15 to 30 minutes, depending on the number of functional groups involved.

different topics handled on different days. A typical sequence of meetings might look like:

- 15 minutes twice per week to review key metrics and improvement activities
- 30 minutes per week to review strategic improvement activities across the value stream
- 1 hour per month for the monthly business review and sharing with senior leadership

HOW TO TIE IN REMOTE TEAMS – ELECTRONIC METHODS

The preferred method of displaying visuals is to make them physical or what is commonly referred to as analog. Analog is making a comeback from everything from books vs. e-books and LP records vs. digital music downloads. Analog visual walls are preferred over their digital counterparts.

The analog is better at capturing the attention of the team and its members, and when trying to drive accountability for improvement in a Lean culture, there is nothing as powerful as posting a sticky with your name on it and then having it displayed all week in plain view in the team area. Every time you walk by the visual board, you are reminded of your commitment to get something done. The persistent, "always on," nature of physical boards drives accountability much better than having items buried in a digital board somewhere. Many teams who started with analog visuals for their process and switched to the digital go back to the analog board. Showing completed items in simple ways, as shown in Figure 9.8, is a powerful way to show that the team is making progress toward continuous improvement.

Still the reality of the modern work means that many office teams have remote participants that connect only through digital means. In these cases, there are many options for digital electronic boards that mimic physical boards. Even with digital visual boards, the desire is to have a persistent image. I recommend to teams that if they must keep a digital board, the board should be displayed in the team area on a monitor and always "be turned on" to remind the team of the commitments for improvements. In

FIGURE 9.8
Improvement tasks completed. There is nothing quite as powerful as showing what the team has accomplished.

reality, what most teams will do is have a blend of analog and digital. For work that is changed and updated throughout the day, hour by hour, or even minute by minute, digital boards help to manage the dynamic nature of the work. However, much of information that is not as dynamic can be shown with physical printouts and updates made by hand right on the printed sheet. Figure 9.9 shows how one Lean team is so attached to its analog boards that they print their spreadsheets each day to show all of the work the team is working on. This team described that it tried to use only digital, but the impact of seeing all of the work in flight, and the priority of what to do next, was lost when the information was kept digitally.

Figure 9.10 is a visual board a team uses to track projects moving through the steps in the value stream. Projects are assigned, and ownership is claimed for the work and shown with a picture of the person working on the task. Boards such as this one can contain a lot of content, and each individual card includes a checklist of reminders for what work needs to be accomplished.

When digital accountability boards are used, as in the case of Figure 9.11, the team still meets at the boards for their daily stand-up meetings. Items are reviewed, but generally the status of the information is updated prior to or after the meeting to save time. A good rule is to

FIGURE 9.9
Daily work printed and displayed on paper to show all the items in flight and their priority. Seeing all of the work in flight everyday has the greatest impact with the team.

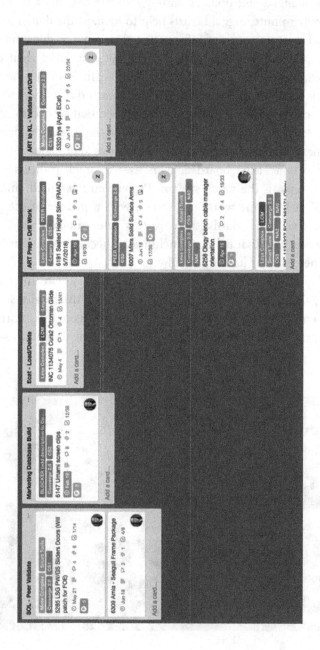

FIGURE 9.10

This customer service team uses an electronic board (using Trello™) to manage the progression of work through the steps in the process.

☐ Advertise the next meetup on MU site	☆
☐ Venue for the next MU?	☆
☐ Debrief / Rvw feedback from last MU	☆
☐ PLAN the next MU's "lesson" portion based on the quarterly rotation in the mtng notice. Guest speaker etc.	☆
☐ Guest Speakers in the future - ask them EARLY	☆
☐ Determine who is going to do what part of agenda?	☆
☐ Review the agenda and tweek	☆

FIGURE 9.11

Accountability items for improvements can be kept in various shared lists. Teams can share lists and track the assignment of tasks. This team uses the shared list capability in Microsoft's Wunderlist™.

never "blind assign" a task to someone who is not at the meeting. Getting commitment to the task from an owner is key to making sure things get done. When items are reviewed and completed, they are checked off the list, and the team does this together. The team should take the opportunity to celebrate and make it a big deal when tasks are completed.

Digital boards also provide a great record of all the past work that has been accomplished. One team uses a digital list to record all of the decisions made by the group. If there is ever a dispute over a decision, the team can go back, review the decision, and see when it was made and who made it. It has become an effective tool to streamline the team meetings.

CASE STUDY – CONNECTING A VALUE STREAM ACROSS A GLOBAL TEAM

Steelcase in Grand Rapids uses remote business centers around the globe to service their customer base around the world. The graphics team is globally dispersed with branches in North America and Romania. The teams track project work across the site. A weekly team meeting keeps the team aligned between multiple sites. Team members use the same list for daily interactions and updates. The status of the work is never in question because the team members claim ownership

D	E	F	G	H	I	J	K	L
Engineering	SmartTools Required (Date)	Assigned To	Validator	Symbol Count	Symbols Complete	Estimated Date Created	Actual Date Created	Validated
YES	NR	VG	NR	4	4	1/31/2018	1/31/2018	1/31/2018
YES	NR	VG	NR	2	2	2/1/2018	2/1/2018	2/1/2018
YES	NR	VG	NR	4	4	2/2/2018	2/2/2018	2/2/2018
NR	NR	VG	NR	1944	1944	2/21/2018	2/21/2018	2/21/2018
YES		GB		418	418	3/19/2018	3/19/2018	
YES	NR	VG		4	4	2/5/2018	2/5/2018	
NR	NR	LC	NR	64	64	2/12/2018	2/12/2018	2/12/2018

FIGURE 9.12
Digital board shared between team members with an online spreadsheet.

or project tasks by putting their initials on the project. The digital visual board is used as a pull system. The digital sharing is accomplished with a shared spreadsheet to which everyone on the team has access. New project work is posted to the board, and team members pull the work as they have capacity to work on it.

In Figure 9.12, the team signals when the information is ready, after engineering work is completed. Green means the entire line is completed. Yellow signifies that additional information needs to be collected. Red tells the team that the project is not ready to be worked on because information is missing.

This pull system creates flow and eliminates a lot of email and wastes in the process. As project work is completed, a fellow team member validates the work. The peer validator marks the line with his or her initials. The teams manage a high volume of projects across multiple time zones and literally across the globe.

SUMMARY

The One Main Thing – Use visual boards across multiple tiers within the organization to build a Lean culture.

STUDY QUESTIONS

1. What is the purpose of visual displays of information in the office?
2. What is a pull system in the office?
3. What is tiered accountability? How is it used to cascade information?
4. What is the typical content of a Tier I visual board?
5. What is the typical content of a Tier II visual board?
6. What is the typical content of a Tier III visual board?
7. How are visual boards used to tie in remote teams?
8. What are the trade-offs to the display of information between analog and digital tools? How are the downsides mitigated?

Section IV

Developing and Sustaining a Lean Culture in the Office

10

The Mature Lean Culture

EDUCATING FOR SELF-SUFFICIENCY IN LEAN

The ultimate goal for Lean implementation is that Lean become embedded in the culture and defines the way the organization behaves and practices every day. The Lean behaviors and habits of continuous improvement come from years of practicing the application of improvement tools with the employees taking the lead in creating improvements on the various systems of the organization. All three levels of the organization have to become involved in the continuous improvement system:

- Upper management and corporate leadership level (sponsorship)
- Management (demonstration and empowerment)
- Teams (active participation)

For teams to actively participate they have to be educated in the various Lean tools. The first place to start is the recognition and elimination of wastes in the value stream. The fact is that employees see many more wastes than their leaders do. They are closest to the problems, and they see process problems and issues every day. The goal in Lean is to have the employees actively involved in spotting wastes and eliminating them.

Lean coaches imbedded within the teams can help employees recognize wastes and make recommendations on ways to eliminate them. The Lean coaches within the organization can be the spark for these efforts. However, the transformation is not the responsibility of them alone. The responsibility for improvement ultimately resides with the teams in the organization.

The transformation must span the entire organization.

TIER III EXECUTIVE AND UPPER LEVEL LEADERS PRACTICE WHAT THEY TEACH

Upper management involvement goes well beyond the set-up of the Lean program. The executive level in the company should use Lean tools to demonstrate their own adoption and support of the Lean system. They need to make connections between functional leaders when value streams cross multiple boundaries. The executive level will also direct the transformation by pointing to areas that need the most improvement. The macro level value stream vantage point helps the teams determine where the most egregious wastes are in the organization, and the leaders point the Lean efforts to focus on these areas. A high level value stream can be shown based on the template shown in Figure 10.1. Understanding the areas to focus on can guide the leaders on which metrics they might focus on for value stream health. Remember that these metrics rarely exist at the highest level; leaders can use tangible, measurable things to predict value stream health and help the staff connect with value stream metrics. These metrics show at a glance how the value stream is operating within its desired window. Trend lines are particularly useful in shown performance over time.

On the leadership team, various "in process" metrics can be displayed to show health. These show how well the value stream is performing against its targets. Trend line charts work well for this purpose. These trends are reviewed frequently on the leadership team. When metrics go red, it is not viewed as bad, but rather as an opportunity for improvement. Each leader on the leadership team works on corrective actions to improve the health of the value stream.

One page, A3 style, documents are displayed to show trends, improvement initiatives, and progress toward strategic goals. The A3 displays on a physical wall are available to anyone on the team. The leadership team should hold monthly and weekly review meetings at the visual wall with their peers and leader. However, the leader may also use the space to hold meetings with the team to reinforce the behaviors and practices of ongoing improvements and to report on value stream metrics. Executive leaders can use the space to understand how various parts of the organization are actually functioning. Gemba walks are common practice for the Lean executives.

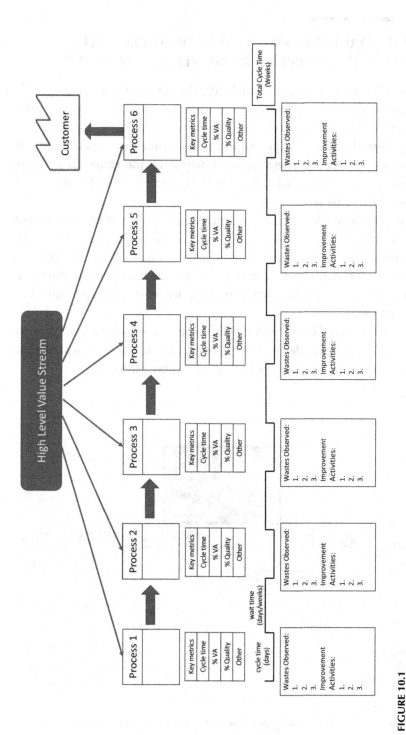

FIGURE 10.1

A visual at the leadership level shows the high-level value stream. it describes wastes observed and strategic improvement activities being worked on to improve the health of the value stream.

TIER II COACHING MANAGERS FOCUS ON VALUE STREAMS AND SUPPORT IMPROVEMENT ACTIVITIES

Mid-level managers are concerned with the day-to-day operation of the various office and administrative value streams. They become most concerned with the improvement of the value streams. Value stream maps allow the team to understand and discuss the value stream. By maintaining a value stream focus and displaying the value stream map, the leader can ensure that there are always activities and assignments surrounding value streams.

These leaders adopt value stream mapping as a way to map out existing work methods and shift them to a new future state. An effective method is to display the high-level value stream in the team area and refer to it often. A visual wall based on the model shown in Figure 10.2 is useful for displaying the value stream and improvement activities.

Kaizens are marked directly on the map. Corresponding A3 project plans are used alongside the value stream map to show improvements. The kaizens A3 plans are reported on in weekly meetings.

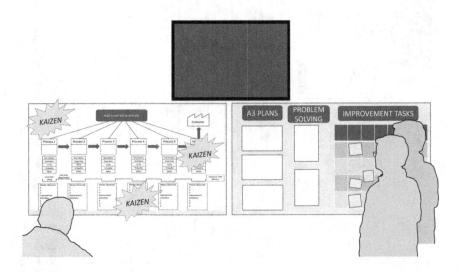

FIGURE 10.2

A Tier II visual board for managers focused on kaizens and improvement activities

It is important for Lean leaders to demonstrate their own dedication to implementing ideas and having their own improvement system. Leaders track issues against value stream health (such as quality and delivery), improvement efforts, and problem-solving root causes and corrective actions. Each item is reported on in the leadership meeting by its owner. These are often tracked on a board like the one shown in Figure 10.3 which give categories for A3 projects, tasks and issues, and 8-step problem solving.

Both the executive leadership team and the managers who report to them are charged with recognizing Lean accomplishments. When teams complete a significant improvement effort, implement an idea of high-impact, or solve a problem with error proofing, the leaders should celebrate with the team. The recognition can take any number of forms, and it should fit in with the culture of the organization. Various ideas for recognizing employees are given in Table 10.1.

LEAN LEADERS FIND THE TRIGGERS FOR LEAN BEHAVIORS

These types of continuous improvement gains need encouragement and support. The leadership team describes and looks for things that will trigger the right Lean behaviors. A trigger can be any problem, issue or value stream gap that needs fixing. The organization needs to recognize what these are; every time one is encountered, the team knows to drive the right corrective action. The triggers in the left

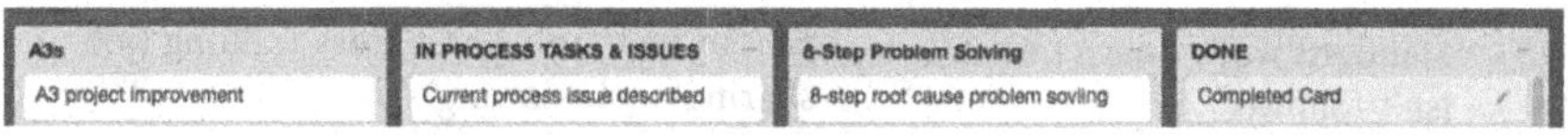

A3s	IN PROCESS TASKS & ISSUES	8-Step Problem Solving	DONE
A3 project improvement	Current process issue described	8-step root cause problem soving	Completed Card

FIGURE 10.3
Typical improvement category headings. 1) A3 project improvements with A3s attached or displayed on a visual board. 2) Value stream health tasks and issues log 3) root cause/corrective action problem solving 4) Done (for logging completed items)

TABLE 10.1

List of Potential Employee Recognitions

Employee Activity	Recognitions
Implement an improvement idea	• Have individual report on idea implemented to the leadership team • Feature in company news • Present a small traveling trophy
Solve an 8-step problem	• Showcase solutions across teams • Have team present the solution to the leadership team
Lead a kaizen	• Gemba walk the kaizen improvements with executives or other leaders
Complete a value stream map	• Print a poster of value stream • Include a team photo • Give lunch or movie tickets

TABLE 10.2

Typical Triggers in an Organization and the Lean Practices They Should Drive

Trigger Events	Lean Behavior and Practices
• Production issues • Customer interruptions • Re-occurring problems • Quality problems • Critical incidents	8-step problem solving with poka-yoke error proofing
• Work doesn't flow but should • Inventory is used to mask problems • Tasks generate rework • Things increase cycle time • Redundant activities • Multiple handoffs	Value stream mapping
• There are Band-Aids or non-effective countermeasures	Develop strong work instructions or training guides
• Standard work doesn't exist or isn't followed	Employee training and cross-training (job sharing or shadowing)

column of Table 10.2 drive the Lean responses shown in the right column.

The leadership team asks for Lean behaviors whenever the trigger conditions exist in the organization. The managers also look for any opportunity to promote further ideas to improve the systems, tools, and work methods.

TIER I – TEAM-BASED IMPROVEMENT SYSTEM

The most powerful activity for accelerating improvement across the organization is the team-based improvement system. This is described in this section, at the end of the book, and tucked away; it should be emphasized. The largest Lean gains are not made by executive-led improvement, by mid-manager value stream projects, or even by black-belt improvement projects. Those account for roughly 20% of the improvements made in an organization. The greatest benefit comes from the improvement ideas implemented by the team. Team-based improvements account for 80% of the improvements generated. The team-based idea system for continuous improvement becomes the driver of change and employee involvement. Since it is such a powerful driver of ongoing continuous improvement, each team should have an idea system governed by the team itself.

The Idea System Basics

There are a variety of idea boards, but most have a simple column system similar to the ones shown in Figure 10.4. These boards live where the team holds stand-up meetings, and they are reviewed often. These are intended to be active boards, with daily movement of sticky notes. The sticky notes move from Capture to To-Do, Doing, and Done. The boards keep a list of idea activators for problems that need to be solved by the team. The team also has a parking lot for ideas that are important to keep track of but can't be worked on right now.

The rules for the board are easy to communicate and follow.

1. Ideas are submitted daily by anyone on the team.
2. Every idea is reviewed in 48 hours by the steering committee.
3. Ideas are divided into fast track (or quick wins) and projects.
4. Bigger projects might be tracked on A3.
5. External resources are pulled in when needed.

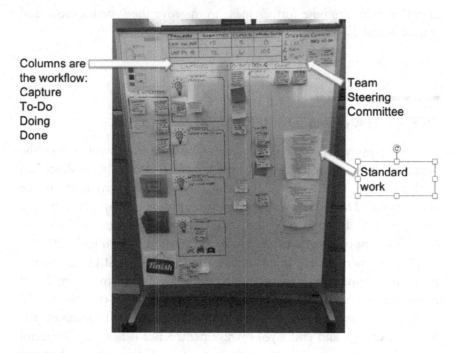

Columns are
the workflow:
Capture
To-Do
Doing
Done

Team
Steering
Committee

Standard
work

FIGURE 10.4
A team-based Tier I idea board

6. Each team tracks implemented ideas and employee participation.
7. Leadership focuses on recognition but not reward$.

The team will use the idea board to work on the problems and wastes they observe in its portion of the value stream. Team members start with problems, contribute ideas to the board, and implement ideas with teammates (note that people often work on ideas other than their own). They ask for help when needed.

Idea Systems Are Led by the Team

The leadership team gives the team the assignment of creating the board, and the leader appoints the initial steering committee. Ideally, the steering committee rotates, with one person going off and another member coming on the committee per month.

Leadership supports the idea system by giving the team members time to work on improvement activities. Leaders, in turn, work on initiating and sustaining the idea system through multiple activities:

- Launch the board with the team
- Appoint the steering committee
- Help the team define the procedures that govern the idea board
- Support its ongoing work
- Empower the team to work on its own problems
- Allow time and energy for working on ideas
- Take on any systemic issues that might bubble up

The employee steering committee is made up of 3 to 4 members from the team. They are the governance for the board and track ideas implemented. They typically meet once per week. The steering committee has several duties:

- Review incoming ideas and ask teammates to work on them
- Keep track of ideas in a log sheet
- Record benefits from each idea (typically stated in hours saved per month)
- Watch for ideas that get stalled and don't move forward

Recognizing Teams for Problem Solving and Implementing Ideas

Remember that the goal for the idea system is 100% participation. Everyone is expected to generate and work on ideas. Robinson and Schroeder report in their work (Idea Driven Organization) – their book and visit to Steelcase inspired the office idea system. That world-class Lean companies implement ideas at a rate of 100 per employee per year. That is 2 implemented ideas per week from everyone in the organization. That level of engagement is remarkable.

Anything the leadership can do to promote the ideas and recognize employees is important. Look for any opportunity to promote the teams that are doing well to the rest of the organization and give individuals credit for implementing new ideas.

Another effective method for getting teams involved in implementing Lean solutions is contests. Having teams submit their best ideas for review by a leadership panel brings recognition to the individuals working on the change. The caveat here is that the Lean contests should not be the only vehicle to create change in the organization. The goal is 100% participation by all employees, and contests limit the participation to the few. A second caveat is to avoid monetary rewards for the contest. Rewarding just a few individuals in the organization for generating and implementing ideas tends to be counterproductive to the goal of getting everyone involved.

CASE STUDY – SMALL GAINS OVER TIME BY A TEAM-RUN IDEA SYSTEM LED TO SIGNIFICANT IMPROVEMENTS

A team that pioneered idea-based continuous improvement in the office showed dramatic improvement after putting the steering committee system in place. After the leader created the steering committee and turned the job of running it over to the team, the results started to dramatically improve. The team of 20 data analysts started to find opportunities for improvements in all corners of its portion of the value stream. The team sustained the system and dramatically improved its own practices.

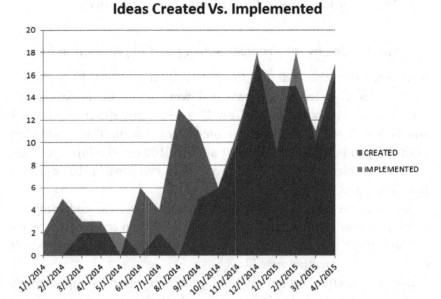

FIGURE 10.5
Results of idea system tracking before and after the steering committee was put in place

For several months at the start of 2014, the idea system was in place, but the steering committee had not yet been formed. The implementation rate of ideas rate was only 2 or 3 ideas per month. After reading the Robinson and Schroeder book *The Idea Driven Organization*, the team generated six times more ideas. With the steering committee in place, the team rapidly implemented ideas. By the end of 2014, the team was implementing over a dozen ideas per month as shown by the graph in Figure 10.5. The team created significant efficiency gains. As its workload increased in 2015, the team found that it could manage the workload without additional staff. This was all due to the ability to implement ideas that created process efficiency improvements. When leadership saw the dramatic improvements made by this team, it decided to expand the idea system across the organization.

SUMMARY

The One Main Thing – Team-led improvement boards rapidly accelerate continuous improvement and achieve 80% of the benefits.

STUDY QUESTIONS

1. What is the behavior that drives the organization toward a Lean culture?
2. What team behavior is desired in a Lean culture for the office?
3. What are the leadership behaviors that drive the organization to adopt Lean as part of their culture?
4. Why is A3 paper used in visual spaces?
5. What should Level II managers do to enable Lean behavior by the teams?
6. How might Level II and III leaders recognize Lean behavior?
7. How are triggers used to drive Lean practices?
8. What is the behavior of Tier I teams in driving improvement?
9. What percentage of improvements is gained from employee initiating improvements?
10. What is the purpose of the Idea Steering Team for the idea system?

11

Sustaining What You Implement

Author's Note: This chapter is primarily for leaders. However, if you are not a leader, keep reading so that you know what Lean expects of the leaders in your organization. Besides, you very well may be a leader in the future, faced with starting or carrying on with a Lean implementation.

INTEGRATING THE SYSTEM WITH YOUR CURRENT LEADERSHIP SYSTEM

Perhaps the most difficult part of Lean in either manufacturing or the office is to sustain the Lean gains. The tendency is for the Lean system to decay and for staff and leadership to revert to their previous fire-fighting behavior. This sustaining behavior mimics placing a wedge behind the ball to keep it from rolling back down the ramp of sustainable Lean behaviors as shown in Figure 11.1. There are many stories of companies who had made impressive gains on the Lean journey, only to decay rapidly once leadership changed their focus to some other initiative. Let's face it. Lean is not habit forming without some care and feeding. The end goal is not to implement a Lean program or set of tools. Instead, the Lean goal is to create a self-sustaining culture. However, many steps and actions sustain Lean and make it an everyday habit.

The Lean initiative needs blocking to keep the forward progress from decaying. If the blocking is removed before reaching the top, the progress is lost as the ball rolls back down the ramp. As each new skill is added, it needs to be supported with leadership activities. The leader needs to build Lean actions into the daily routine as the team forms habits of daily Lean behavior. With time and proper leadership support,

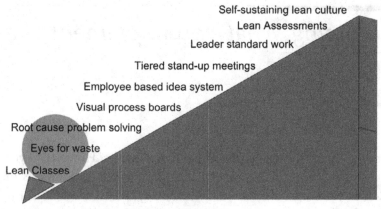

Sustaining Lean

Self-sustaining lean culture
Lean Assessments
Leader standard work
Tiered stand-up meetings
Employee based idea system
Visual process boards
Root cause problem solving
Eyes for waste
Lean Classes

Leaders are the teachers and coaches

FIGURE 11.1

Sustaining Lean requires following a series of steps in a journey. Once the ball gets to the top it will roll on its own.

the Lean system needs will become part of the practice and habit of how the organization operates on a daily basis.

I was recently in an organization that had implemented one tool into the production system. A pitch-tracking chart was displayed near each machine. The charts had been put in place by a previous Lean effort. As I examined the boards, only about a third of them were up to date on first shift, and the second shift had in stopped using them all together in every work center. The operators that were still using them seemed to be going through the motions. The problem was that the information stopped with the operators. To the operator's credit, they were tracking pitch attainment and even writing on the boards the reasons for misses. However, the information gathering stopped with the operators, and any awareness of the root causes of the missed pitch ended with the operators. The next layer of analysis, pareto chart, or corrective action at the line supervisor level was totally absent.

In the office, a similar opportunity exists to capture errors, rework, and quality issues as they happen. If these stop with the knowledge workers, and don't become actionable with corrective action behavior, then the same fate will reach the office as the plant floor. The Lean initiative will decay. To avoid the decay and backsliding, issues need to be captured and worked on when they are found with continuous improvement efforts. The next level of leadership must also be active in the system. The leaders also must be looking for opportunities to direct the teams to work on continuous improvements in the value streams in the organization.

OWNING THE INITIATIVE – IT BEGINS AND MAINTAINS WITH ENGAGED LEADERS

Leaders are the sustaining factor in Lean implementations. Leaders need to practice their own continuous improvement and constantly help the organization work on improving the value streams. Leaders are always scanning the horizon of work steps and systems candidates looking for prime candidates for improvement. Leaders don't back away from systematic projects that need to be completed to improve the value streams.

The best Lean leader practices Lean at work and at home. What does this look like? The Lean leader is attempting to remove waste from his or her own personal workflow. The leaders use their own meeting time to launch and review improvement activities. Lean leaders listen for clues for what's broken in the value stream and then propose changes to make improvements. Leaders make sure that the team has the skills and time to work on problems. Here are the key behaviors that should be reinforced in a Lean office culture:

- Root-cause problem solving becomes the repeatable practice when the organization encounters a problem or a hiccup.
- Value stream mapping is used to fix cross-functional issues.
- Waste becomes the focus of office-improvement efforts.
- Employees are involved in solving problems.
- Every member of the staff is generating improvement ideas and working to implement them.
- Rework is measured and becomes the enemy of leadership.
- People in the organization are taught the skills for continuous improvement.

The most effective organizations have embedded Lean practices into their regular activities in order to sustain their Lean efforts. Their weekly and daily team meetings reserve time for updates on value stream health and take the time to discuss improvements needed to shore up the work steps and standards.

LEADERS TAKE REGULAR OFFICE VALUE STREAM GEMBA WALKS AND ASK GREAT QUESTIONS

Many organizations have conditioned their collective brains to filter out the wastes. They have become tolerant and numb to the wastes in the value streams. They put Band Aids on the same things over and over, but the same issues reappear. In most organizations, leaders are too content with putting out fires and put all of their effort there.

Why does this happen? The brain has a tendency to block things out, and we learn to react to some things while ignoring others. For instance, a person can learn to sleep through loud noises. The brain allows us to block out noises when we learn that there is no consequence of the noises. Science discovered in the 1960s that the brain can block out many things and then focus on only what it knows is important. The researchers found a center in the brain called the reticular formation that is a supreme filter for information. The research explains why a mother will not wake up when a loud truck travels down the road while she is sleeping, especially if the passing truck is a regular occurrence, but will hear the baby's cry in the next bedroom and wake up. The brain determines that the truck is a common event and not one to cause worry. However, the baby's cry means that the baby needs attention. Its diaper needs to be changed or the baby is hungry, and the parent jumps into action.

Our brains have become numb to the wastes in the value streams in the office. We dismiss the problems as things that have always been that way or believe that they are unsolvable. If Lean is nothing else, it is a system for making us see the wastes to the point that we will no longer let our brains ignore them.

In a similar way, the Lean thinker has to retrain his or her brain to recognize and remove wastes that have been commonplace in the organization. Leaders look for problems verbalized from the teams and train their eyes to see the wastes.

In Lean, the practice of going to the Gemba is a way to see the wastes. However, an office Gemba looks quite different from one in manufacturing where the wastes unfold in real time as you watch the parts flow down the value stream. In the office, since the work is buried in computers, the work steps and the wastes in and between the steps are hidden from view. Earlier, we discussed the importance of value stream mapping the work steps for this very reason. The other Lean practice for leaders to embrace is regularly walking the office value stream, looking for wastes.

What does Gemba walking look like in the office?

The leader, or in this case, the Gemba walker does the following:

- Start as close to the beginning as possible, which is typically the step or set of steps that are closest to the customer.
- Interview the workers and have them show you what they do on a daily basis. This involves asking them to show you the actual work they are doing, right down to the individual computer screens on which they interact with data.
- Ask them about the transition of work in and out:

  o Where do the inputs come from?
  o What is the incoming quality of their inputs? (Do they ever send it back for rework?)
  o To whom do they hand their work?

- Ask the workers where they see wastes:

  o What wastes have they observed?
  o What bugs them about their part of the overall value stream?
  o What bugs them about other work steps? (A word of caution here: You might have to remind them that you are focused on the work steps, and not the workers. These two need to be separated to avoid creating a complaint session against fellow workers. This is not part of Lean, which always seeks respect for people).

With a 20- to 30-minute stop at each person in the workflow, the leader can quickly assess how well the system is functioning. If there are problems, the leader elevates these to opportunities for improvements and makes someone on the team or the leadership team accountable for solving these problems.

It is always a good idea for the leader to take a trained set of eyes along on the Gemba walk. A Lean sensei, who might be an internal Lean expert or an external expert, can help the leader recognize waste and ask the right questions to follow the flow (or find the lack of flow) in the value stream.

VISUAL BOARDS FOR THE ACTIVE LEADER PARTICIPANT DISPLAY PROCESS HEALTH

The core tools in the Lean box are the visual boards used to check on the value stream health to field problems that have been observed and assign ownership to work on them. When a professional baseball player takes the field, the area for which he is responsible to catch the ball and make the play is already very clear to him. Many balls hit to the outfielder need no clarification. They are clearly hit in the outfielder's territory. Yet, there are many cases when the ball is in a grey zone between the outfielders or between the outfield and the infield. In these cases, players "call for" the ball. The same is true in fielding problems in Lean. The purpose of the accountability visual boards is to make clear who owns the problems and who is working on them.

The leaders Gemba walk by regularly attending the stand-up meetings at the visual boards. The leaders ask the team:

- Are the problems being raised to the team?
- Who is calling "this one is mine"?
- Are things driving to completion?
- What can I do to help?

This simple leader behavior is very effective in ensuring that a culture of continuous improvement is being built across the organization.

EMPHASIZE THE LEAN PRINCIPLES AND CUSTOMIZE THEM TO YOUR ORGANIZATION

The Lean principles can be integrated seamlessly with the strategic initiatives at the leadership level. The Lean principles can also be easily taught and understood. The 5 basic principles are clearly articulated and shared in all communications and while educating the employees on what it means to be Lean. Some companies choose to take the Lean principles and customize them to their own language. This is an effective means of internalizing the Lean methodology. The 5 principles of Lean don't change, but they may need translation to your organization. Table 11.1 provides space for recording your ideas for translating the Lean principle into language relevant to your organization.

The strategies for continuous improvement should be visible throughout the organization. Everyone from the executives to the front desk should understand the Lean message and the emphasis on continuous improvement. The Lean strategy becomes an important element in the leadership Lean space. The various Lean initiatives must be owned by the leadership. Each principle should be endorsed by the leaders. Leaders should teach the Lean principles.

The best way for the organization to learn and do Lean is for the leadership to teach, promote, and coach the organization on the principles of Lean. The leaders should teach the principles of Lean even before the tools. In fact, the Lean concepts are simple to learn. They are however, difficult to master. The best way to tackle and sustain a Lean implementation is to start with the principles.

Changing the culture means changing behavior and habits. Leadership needs to adopt the Lean philosophy. All levels from the CEO, president, vice president, directors, managers, and staff need to adopt a continuous improvement mindset. In this mindset, everything can be improved. Every system can be made more efficient and transformed into something better.

TABLE 11.1

Translate the Lean Principles into Your Organization's Language

Lean Principle	Translate the Principles to Your Organization
Seek customer value first	
Eliminate wastes	
Make work flow	
Leadership involvement	
Seek perfection (you're never done)	

Even systems that have been looked at in the past have room for improvement. Remember the 50% rule. Assume there is 50% waste in any value stream and that significant improvements can always be made. Each individual in the organization and every leader have to own the continuous improvement within their own piece of the larger value stream. There is a saying in Lean that "The future state becomes the next current state." This restlessness and constant emphasis on improvement becomes the mantra of the leadership and staff alike.

This means also that teams are empowered to make changes to their own part of the value stream. This requires a different type of leadership. A Lean leader cannot be command-and-control (or hierarchical) type of leader. If the leader is involved in every change, and has to approve every improvement proposal, the pace of change will be bogged down, driving momentum to zero. Instead, the Lean leader relinquishes control to the team who develops its own best practices based on the principles and tools in Lean.

Lean leaders are always looking for the Lean champions and change agents emerging in the organization. They will be the next Lean advocates. Often, they will be active participants in kaizens and improvement workshops, and the leaders tap on them to think about the next transformation.

The qualities of a Lean champion were listed described in detail in Chapter 3 (See Table 3.2). Here once again is the list of the qualities to look for in emerging Lean leaders. A Lean champion is the following:

1. A person who has a passion for and intense commitment to Lean
2. A person who is willing to be a change agent and is impatient with the status quo
3. An individual who can teach one on one or in small groups
4. A person who can think on his or her feet
5. Someone who is comfortable in front of leaders and executives
6. An individual who has a high tolerance for ambiguity and uncertainty
7. An individual who applies these concepts to any team and in personal life

LEADER STANDARD WORK IN THE OFFICE

Leader standard work in the office has the same purpose as it does in Lean manufacturing. The Lean leader builds in daily and weekly

TABLE 11.2

Leader Standard Work for the Office

Mark When Completed	Daily Activities	Notes for Follow-up/Opportunities for Improvement
☐	Attend team stand-up (Tier I) meeting	
☐	Review accountability board for improvements	
☐	Attend leader's continuous improvement (Tier II) meeting	
☐	Weekly activities	
☐	Look for triggers (problems) that might require root-cause problem solving	
☐	Meet with upstream leader in the value stream	
☐	Meet with downstream leader in the value stream	
☐	Attend team idea steering committee meeting	
☐	Update trend metrics on the leader visual board	
☐	Update your own A3 improvement activities	
☐	Train and coach team as needed in Lean principles and tools	

routine activities (as shown in Table 11.2) that will support and sustain Lean implementation. The standard work can be part of the leader's calendar, or it can be a checklist that the leader follows on a daily basis.

The list contains activities that the leader does on a regular basis to sustain Lean implementation. Leader standard work is highly customizable to each leader and his or her duties.

USING ASSESSMENTS

Lean assessments are just as effective in the office as in manufacturing for determine the progress made toward a mature Lean culture over time. After all, what gets measured gets done. Table 11.3 lists the 8 Lean dimensions for assessing the Lean culture change for the office. If there is a clear measurement of progress on the Lean journey, then there can

TABLE 11.3

Lean Assessment Chart

Dimensions of Office Lean	Rating (1-5)	Comments
1 Value stream mapping		
2 Visual boards		
3 Daily accountability		
4 Process definition		
5 Process discipline		
6 Continuous improvement		
7 Problem solving		
8 Job instruction and training		

be a truly objective evaluation of how your organization is doing. The assessment follows the 8 dimensions that are critical to any Lean implementation. These allow the organization to do a self-assessment against the standards of a fully developed Lean culture.

Table 11.4 shows the values for rating each of the 8 dimensions on a scale of 1 to 5, from pre-implementation (1) to a sustainable system (5). The rating scale follows the progression in maturity from pre-implementation to sustaining the Lean system and culture.

TABLE 11.4

The Rating Scale for Assessing Progress toward a Sustainable Lean Culture

Rating	Level of Implementation	Description
1	Pre-implementation	Evidence of skill or tool is not yet observed in the organization.
2	Implementation	Evidence of the skill or tool can be observed in pockets within the organization, and a few people demonstrate the behavior.
3	First recognizable state	Evidence of the skill or tool is observed in many areas, and leaders and champions practice the skill independently.
4	System stabilizing	The skills and tools are used throughout the organization, and there are many people with the skills.
5	Sustainable system	The skills and tools are common practice and used independently without coaching or teaching.

By assessing all 8 dimensions, one can create before and after images in relation to progress. The best assessments are those the team owns and completes itself. A self-assessment is the most powerful. The gaps between where the team is and where it wants to be can drive additional continuous improvement initiatives inside the company. An example of before and after ratings on each of the 8 dimensions is shown in Figure 11.2.

Some teams might object to having an outside assessment. Indeed, it can be intimidating and even a little demoralizing. A better approach is to have the leaders and team assess the Lean initiative for themselves. The score is not the end goal. For each dimension, the comments are even more important because they will point the team toward the improvements that they should be making. The best assessments are those the team owns and completes.

The Lean assessment chart in Table 11.3 has a third column for taking notes as to the reason for the rating. These comments will help the leader and team determine appropriate next actions on the Lean journey.

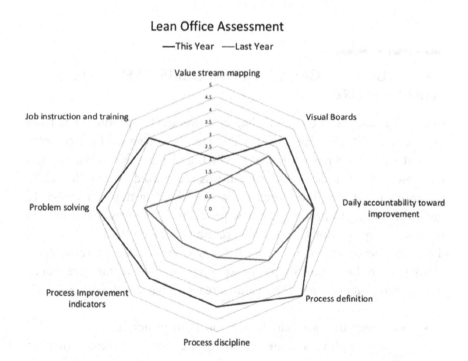

FIGURE 11.2
A spider or radar chart used to assess progress from one period to the next on the journey to Lean excellence.

A LEAN OFFICE CULTURE – A POWERFUL ENGINE

The end goal in the journey of a Lean transformation is to have a self-sustaining system. At this point, all of the dimensions are in place. At the heart of Lean, there is a self-sustaining improvement system, where both the leaders and the team are constantly working to improve the systems. The leaders are taking the time for improvement, and they are encouraging the teams to do the same. One of the things that I love to do is observe people and teams who "get it." These people have caught the Lean bug and are actively improving their systems. I can always tell which individual leaders and groups are actively pursuing Lean because their system today looks different than it did the last time it was observed. If a system has not changed in a week or a couple of months, that is a clear indicator that the improvements are not being pursued. On the other hand, if there are observable changes for the better (definition of kaizen), then you know that the team is moving forward on the Lean journey.

CASE STUDY – A GROUP TRANSFORMS ITSELF INTO A LEAN CULTURE

In the case study at the end of Chapter 2, we saw the product data team as they started their Lean journey. The team was plagued by a complex current state in which work was batched, had many handoffs, and did not flow at all. The data value stream was recognized as a bottleneck in the company. It took more time to develop the data than it required to build the tooling to produce the new products. There was well over 50% rework, many handoffs, and many redundancies built in to track the data. Let's fast forward to a dozen years later in their journey. After many years of Lean workshops and kaizen events, the teams have placed many Lean practices into their value stream. What are the differences?

- Team members are fully trained on Lean principles.
- As new employees come on board, they are also trained in Lean principles.
- All of the value streams at macro and individual team levels have been mapped, and kaizen improvements have been put in place.

- The teams complete their own root-cause problem solving on any issues that come up.
- Instead of one large batch, the teams now work in a flow. Projects are discussed weekly in a large team meeting, and a visual board shows all projects in flight.
- The rework has gone down well below 5%, and now individual rework incidents are rare; if they do come up, the team works to resolve the issues.
- Each sub-team has its own idea system and actively suggests additional ways to improve its portion of the value stream: After all, you are never done with continuous improvement.
- The management team has its own Tier II visual board and deals with systematic issues at its level.

The team is now much more productive. At one point, it estimated that it was easily out-producing its old batch methods by over 40%. Lean has worked, and it is a self-sustaining system. The team frequently hosts customer groups who want to see Lean in action, and it is a showcase for Lean in the office.

SUMMARY

The One Main Thing – Leadership sustains the Lean implementation until it becomes self-sustaining.

STUDY QUESTIONS

1. What is the ultimate end goal for a Lean program?
2. What is the leader's role in supporting the Lean progress made?
3. What is the countermeasure to decay in the Lean system?
4. What are behaviors of an engaged Lean leader?
5. What have effective Lean organizations regularly done to sustain Lean?
6. Why does the organization become conditioned to overlook wastes?

7. What can be done in order to uncover more wastes in the value streams of the organization?

8. What does Gemba walking look like in the office?

9. What is a key activity for leaders to perform to sustain Lean?

10. What is the purpose of leader standard work in the office?

11. How and why are Lean assessments used in the office?

12

Lean Strategy in the Office

CASCADING STRATEGIC ACTIVITIES

As the Lean implementation matures, the organization will see the opportunity to link Lean strategic initiatives to the corporate strategy. The efforts to continually improve office value streams can be integrated into the strategy of the organization. This connection makes sense and provides a method to encourage everyone to be involved in continuous improvement. It will greatly leverage the ability for the whole organization to get behind the Lean movement. Lean, continuous improvement can become a central transformational theme within an organization.

Strategies cascade from the upper levels in the organization down to the managers and teams. Strategy is linked between leadership levels using a Lean method called Hoshin-Kanri (roughly translated as "policy management"), the goal of which is to define the compass direction for the organization. In Lean, this direction-setting method is often referred to as defining the "true north" for the organization, by which the organization can navigate and steer. It is the long-term direction that does not falter or waiver. It is both aspirational and challenging.

To one on the seas, celestial navigation is accomplished by measuring the angle from the horizon to the North Star, which in turn gives the latitude position of the vessel. This method depends on the fact that the North Star is always directly over the North Pole. This true north allows navigation to take place.

In a similar way, the true north of the Lean program needs to be defined as the never-changing goal of the organization. The organizational North Star in Lean will include multiple components:

1. continuous improvement to work toward ultimate perfection
2. solving problems and root-cause elimination by all in the organization
3. eliminating all wastes
4. respecting and developing people
5. involving everyone in improving the value stream

Key items that are often linked to the strategic vision are:

- Development of leaders and staff with skills surrounding Lean
- Leader support of the Lean initiative and efforts by teams toward continuous improvement
- Improving quality through the use of root-cause problem solving
- Individual and team based continuous improvement idea systems
- Continuous improvement efforts by teams with error proofing (poka-yoke)
- Connecting work processes across the value stream
- Making the value stream visual to show its health
- New LEAN continuous improvement projects, kaizens, with A3s project plans

MEASURING FOR VALUE STREAM IMPROVEMENTS

The Lean value stream metrics give the organization a way to measure improvement initiatives. These leading metrics are indicators that tell how the value stream is operating at this moment in time. Lean metrics do not look back on the performance of last month or last quarter. Lean metrics show the status of the value stream at any given hour in the day. This is a dramatic difference from traditional reporting metrics. It also represents a significant cultural difference in how the organization measures itself.

> The primary purpose of visual measures in Lean: show the current condition of the value stream from the customer's perspective.

In other words, the visuals have to show the status of the value stream today. For example, as I wrote this book, I used a chart showing which chapters and figures were completed on any given day. That allowed me to see if I was ahead or behind schedule to reach the due date for the completed manuscript. Lean metrics progress toward a goal and allow the organization to react if they miss plan. Missing plan is merely a topic of discussion in Lean for finding ways to put the plan back on track.

REPORTING ON PROGRESS

What makes Lean metrics different is the idea that teams measure the status of their own work as it relates to the performance of the overall value stream. Various measures include daily status updates (stand-up meetings) on various categories:

- Quality metrics – the Lean metric that will show the status of the quality of the current work against a standard
- Cycle time metrics (throughput) – a measure that will show how long the current work spends in the value stream vs. the goal for that work to finish
- Processing time metrics (capacity) – a measure of the amount of work content for the current work against the goal or historical averages for that work
- Service metrics (response time) – a measure of the current customer response time versus the goal
- Continuous improvement metrics – shows the current improvement activities in flight including value stream mapping workshops, A3 project plans, root-cause problem solving, kaizens, etc.
- Employee involvement metrics (training and ideas implemented) – shows how many employees have been trained in Lean methods and concepts and how many are actively involved in submitting and working on improvement ideas across the organization

Notice that all of these metrics report on the activities in flight. They are not metrics that measure last quarter or last month. Wherever possible, they show the current condition of the area being measured.

GETTING LEADERSHIP INVOLVED IN ITS OWN IMPROVEMENTS

The leadership team will become directly involved in reporting on the metrics in its weekly and monthly sessions. The leadership adopts its own improvement initiatives based on the observed metrics. The leader's job is to demonstrate improvement at his or her level in the organization to show support for the Lean methods to the teams. In order to accomplish this, the leaders need their own stand up with its own stand-up agenda as depicted in Table 12.1.

Author's Note: One the manufacturing side of the business, the strategy is typically to link Lean strategic improvements through the categories of safety, quality, delivery, and cost (SQDC). Of these four categories, three transfer well to the office, but Safety typically does not work well in the office. What is safety when people are sitting at desks? Safety might be interpreted as the readiness to react to natural disasters such as hurricanes or tornados. This is important of course, and it should be part of the organization's disaster recovery plans. In Lean, a better interpretation of safety in the office might be risk. Here the idea is to reduce or eliminate risks to the business due to anything from competition, technology, the marketplace, or the environment (which includes readiness for natural disasters). When the risks are part of the strategic plan, they drive their own improvement initiatives. Risks may also be represented by the tensions on the teams. These tensions come into play when the organization is trying to move forward but the

TABLE 12.1

Typical Leadership Stand-Up Agenda for Continuous Improvement (Multiple Times Per Week)

Leadership Stand-Up Agenda
Review quality issues with current work and list corrective actions
Review late projects from visual board
Review high volume work and staffing
Give status updates on improvement projects in flight
Review any open issues and actions
Complete root-cause problem solving for repeating production issues
Round table

tension is holding them back. For example, a team faced with an aging software system would share the tradeoff of the cost of upgrade versus the potential interruption to the business (and the loss of productivity and revenue).

CASE STUDY – A LEADERSHIP GEMBA SPACE DRIVES STRATEGY AND IMPROVEMENT

Leaders in the Product Data group at Steelcase display their strategy in the team area where all can see. The "Gemba space" or "obeya room" (translated from the Japanese as "big room"), is a space that displays the strategy for the organization and drives the strategy down to the managers and teams. The strategy and metrics are prominently displayed at all times to create transparency from the leaders to the teams. The leaders meet twice per week in their own stand-up meeting to discuss leading metrics in risks, quality, delivery, and cost. There is an active discussion around the improvements that are being made and those that need to be made to the process.

The leadership shows and tracks improvement metrics at their own visual board as illustrated in Figure 12.1. They assign ownership for improvement activities and reports on trends in the leading metrics. Below the main strategy board are a number of key metrics each manager is tracking. Each metric has a clear green/red indicator. Figure 12.2 shows a typical leadership trend graph with a clearly indicated red status and follow-up action items. Red is not to be avoided in a Lean culture. Instead, red is embraced by the leadership team as an opportunity to work on a process problem. Each metric has a spot on the bottom to indicate the current status of the metric.

When the metrics reveal a quality issue, the management team launches a root-cause problem solving activity with the team. The teams are often asked to report the results of the analysis and the plans to correct the situation to the leadership team. Also, any type of error proofing (or poka-yoke) is highly celebrated. The management team is also actively involved in launching value stream workshops on their teams.

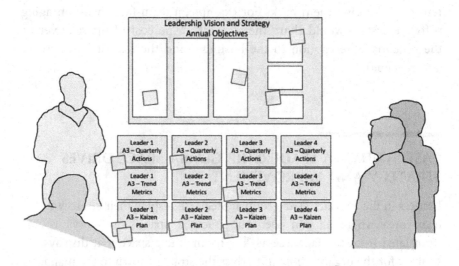

FIGURE 12.1

The leadership team meets at a strategy board. Leadership discusses actions, current trends, and improvement activities. Note the use of sticky notes to dynamically update the direction.

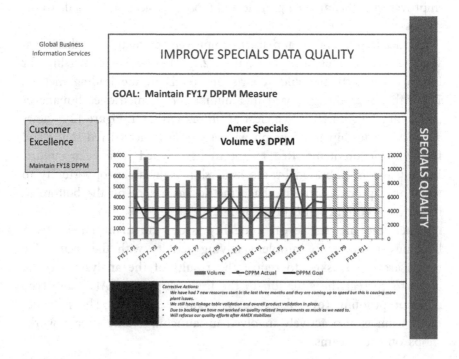

FIGURE 12.2

Trend metrics carry a red/green indicator. If a metric is red, then the corrective action is filled in, which triggers the improvement activities to improve the metric.

SUMMARY

The One Main Thing – The primary purpose of visual measures in Lean is to show the current condition or health of the value stream from the customer's perspective.

STUDY QUESTIONS

1. What is the concept of setting true north for the organization?
2. What are common elements of true north for a Lean program?
3. What is the primary purpose of measuring the value stream performance?
4. What is the leader's role with respect to value stream measures?

13

Lean, Development, and Agile

FIVE WAYS LEAN PREPARES TEAMS FOR AGILE WAYS OF WORKING

Agile is the hot new work process, and it's difficult to ignore. With a work methodology that boasts productivity improvements, enhanced effectiveness, and fulfilling work for its team members, it seems like a panacea. The danger, of course, with any new work approach is to "throw the baby out with the bathwater" and assume that the best new work systems are better than anything that came before. In addition, agile brings a requirement for us to learn an innovative system of working and figure out how best to support it. This is no small challenge given our already full-to-overflowing workloads.

The good news is that history is a guide, and agile isn't so vastly different from the effectiveness of Lean methodologies we have looked at in this book. Lean started in the factory, and we have shown how it can be adapted and translated into the office.

It's a new day, however, with agile taking hold in IT and expanding to all kinds of work beyond software development.[1] Far from methodologies that apply only in manufacturing or in IT, these work approaches can enlighten us in some of the most effective ways of working – for all kinds of work. Here are some of the lessons learned.

Focus on the Customer[2]

Definition: In Lean, the focus is on and the value is defined by the customer. Takt time is the rate at which new work needs to be produced, and faster isn't better. The ideal is to produce work at the pace the customer demands it. Similarly, agile starts with story cards written from the customer's point of view and based on the customer's criteria for success. A key expectation of the product owner (the customer representative in agile) is to embed with the team and stay deeply connected to the work of the team. In addition, the product owner's role is to be a liaison with the business owner and other stakeholders. Show and tell sessions at the conclusion of each sprint provide the opportunity for the team to report to the customer on the progress and the value the team has created in that portion of the work.

Lesson: This enduring theme of customer first, customer embeddedness, and customer centrality is surely a lesson for our work. I used to work with a leader who said regularly, "If you're not serving the end customer, you'd better be serving someone who is."

One Thing at a Time

Definition: A hallmark of agile is to work on one project at a time with team members who are present and focused on the tasks that must be completed in order to accomplish the sprint. With Lean, a method called one-piece flow ensured that there was no batching (doing things in groups) and that each piece flowed through the system one at a time so that value was added for each piece on its path to the customer. Both agile and Lean endeavor to reduce the work in process (or WIP) and enable the flow of the work.

Lesson: In our multitasking world where it's hard to process issues or get to decisions because everyone is focused on so many different projects, doing one thing at a time is not only a welcome relief, but increasingly is the only way work will get done effectively.

Visual Displays

Definition: In Lean, workplaces "leverage" kanban boards, visual displays, and dashboards, with the intention of managing work visually and providing a place teams could see the status of their work at a glance. Agile is similar with daily standups held around work authorization and kanban boards. Teams within information technology hold quick meetings around their analog boards, and following the meeting the scrum master or project manager has 10 minutes within which to update the digital version of the board so that it is accessible physically and virtually to all team members.

Lesson: Make work visual and visible so that everyone can be aware of the work, its status, and the shared processes that must be accomplished.

Continuous Improvement

Definition: In Lean, we are taught to look for non-value-added work and root it out (we identified the work that didn't add value for the customer, as the "8 wastes"). In every process, we started with the assumption that there was 50% waste in things like movement, inventory, over-processing, and the like. In a similar vein, the agile retrospective focuses on feedback, learning, and continuous improvement at the conclusion of every sprint.

Lesson: We are all moving fast, and this speed frequently gets in the way of our taking the time to reflect, regroup, and systematically identify areas for improvement. Without this learning, we undermine progress and growth. It is counterintuitive, but agile teaches us that to pause and reflect actually helps us speed up because of the improvement that occurs.

Empowered Leaders Empower Teams

Finally, both Lean and agile feature the best of leadership and team theory. Across multiple disciplines, industries, and situations, leadership is most effective when it is shared and emergent. Those with knowledge on key topics are empowered to influence others, and decision-making is distributed. Cross-trained team members and a focus on avoiding specialization and breaking down "towers of knowledge" allow for development of skills and more fluidity in moving from one job to the next and more flexibility in getting the work done. Teams are empowered to direct their own work and provide each other with feedback. The leader is guide and coach to a team that is both enabled with skills and empowered to implement them in creating value for the customer.

In the early days of Lean, there was a story that circulated about Toyota and its world-renown production systems. They were said to regularly allow their competitors to tour their plants, see their processes, and take pictures and plenty of notes. When one of their competitors asked why they allowed this kind of openness, they said confidently there was no risk in competitors seeing their processes today because they would all be different by tomorrow. This was the nature of empowered teams constantly improving with a focus on the customer and a rigorous approach to constant improvement. This was the power of their process, which shares the same fundamentals of agile.

While agile may be the newest thing we're scrambling to learn, implement, and employ, it is significantly informed by all that came before. Rather than a nod to the future that calls the past into question, it is building on all the learning we've done over the years.

JUMP STARTING DEVELOPMENT THROUGH IMPROVEMENT PROJECTS

When it comes to the development process itself, a different set of Lean methods is used. The author's previous book, *Innovative Lean Development* (Productivity Press © 2010), describes the practice of using fast learning cycles in development. In the early conceptual stages of development work, a special iterative process is required. In the early stages of development, knowledge and understanding are missing. During the conceptual phase, knotty problems with complex tradeoffs need to be solved. At this stage, rapid bursts of learning are used to solve knotty problems that in turn generate new knowledge.

In Lean, flow is described as working on one thing at a time. The backlog of things that have to be worked on is clearly listed and prioritized. In development, the work to be done is in the form of knowledge gaps and things that must be learned. When these are properly organized and prioritized in the backlog, the team can pick things to work on next. This is so much better than trying to work on everything at once. These fast learning cycles are a follow-on to the idea of limiting the work in process (WIP) to make work flow. Figure 13.1 depicts breaking knowledge and discovery work into learning cycles. A similar goal exists in agile, where teams manage the story cards in the work backlog and then work on a limited set of story cards in the current agile sprint.

The development process at nearly every organization in the world follows a pre-defined process, which is called a phase gate process. The phase gate process assumes one long slow learning cycle. A typical phase gate process map would look like this:

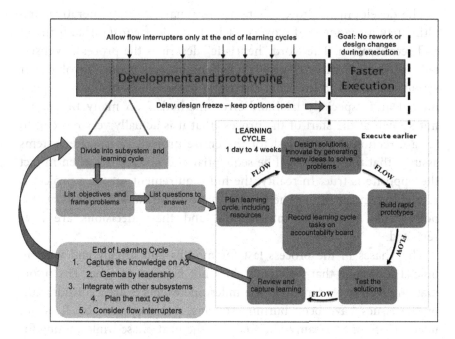

FIGURE 13.1
Lean learning cycles create flow of knowledge Reference Schipper and Swets. AME Target Magazine. First Issue, 2010.

Typical Phase Gate Process
    Concept →
        Requirements definition →
            Exploration →
                Design →
                    Testing →
                        Execution →
                            Life cycle management
Duration of each phase is typically months

The basic problem with the phase gate approach is that it is a push system and does not allow the work to flow. It does not allow much room for trial and error or re-planning, since it assumes that a complete and accurate set of requirements can be known up front, which is rarely true.

The development process is by its very nature messy, iterative, and ultimately a matter of discovery. It is in need of constant adjustment and recalibration. The word "heuristic" describes the process. Webster tells us that a "heuristic" problem solving process is one "involving or serving as an aid to learning, discovery, or problem-solving by experimental and especially trial-and-error methods." So many things are not known at the start of the process that it is actually very difficult to set a direction that will last for the entire project. Phase gate systems assume that the phases will be sequential and not repeat, when in fact the opposite is true. In reality, the full requirement set for a project is rarely known up front. The team is typically making decisions at this point with incomplete information, and these decisions are later revisited.

The phases in the process last for months and usually end with an official milestone that frequently does not happen on time. The information given to leadership at the milestone events is aged considerably, or the issues have been burning so long that they are hot. It is not uncommon for the team to be well into the next phase while waiting for the official "milestone meeting" to occur and for decisions to be made. The milestones do not inform design changes in a timely manner. If changes in direction are required at the milestone, there can be significant rework to the project. Generally, the team has so much invested in the design that it becomes very difficult to turn back and reset the project. A different method of quick feedback and agility to adjust the course is needed.

What is different about Lean and agile? Very early in the project, the team creates a list of all of the work that needs to be done and keeps it in a backlog, but the backlog undergoes continual grooming by the product owner. The team then pulls work from the backlog. The team keeps a large visual board that displays all of the work that must be completed. In Lean terminology, this visual wall is a giant kanban or pull system. Work is prioritized and placed in order with respect to importance and inter dependencies. The planning board is kept up to date throughout the stages of the project. The board informs the team as to what items have been closed and which ones still need to be closed. Even more important is that the team is constantly adjusting the plan to ensure the right things are worked on.

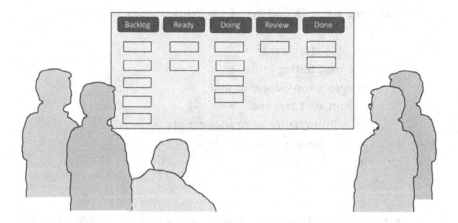

FIGURE 13.2

An agile visual board displays the work backlog and work in process. It includes prioritized work in the backlog that is ready to start, and all work that is in process. Color dots are used to indicate the current status of the work. The board is often analog, even when the team members are doing digital work at their computers.

The plan remains fluid. You might say that the ink is always wet on the paper of the plan. When planning and working with the team, the visual board always describes the current status of the development plan. A good visual board will show the work waiting to start, that in process, and that completed. Figure 13.2 illustrates the typical agile visual board, which is often referred to as a Kanban board. If any work is blocked, then it is shown with a red dot. The visual indicator shows the team and its leadership the status of work in real time. The team reports any issues up to the leaders, and they can be quickly handled.

Just as in the culture of Lean, in agile red is not bad or to be avoided. Instead, a red dot on a piece of work in agile shows that the work is simply stuck. Either the piece of work is not well defined, or there is something wrong outside the team preventing it from moving forward.

When functioning well, the visual board should be able to show at a glance the status of the current work in the project. There is always a clear indication of how many different pieces of work are in process along with their expected finish dates. Any work that is not yet started should be clearly visible in the work backlog.

Typical Agile Cycle in Software Development:
Plan →
    Review user story cards →
        Write unit testing code →
           Programming done in pairs →
                Run unit test code →
                    Run quality assurance scripts →
                  Review with the client
Duration – 1 or 2 weeks

In software development, agile cycles, called sprints, allow a much larger project to be broken down into smaller 1- or 2-week cycles. When the cycles become the focus, and everyone in the organization works in concert to maintain the cadence, then the pattern is repeatable and sustainable. In this way, the team is creating flow by limiting the WIP and ensuring the cycles can be repeated. The number of cycles (or sprints in agile) that have been completed along with the amount of work completed in each one is clearly displayed by the team. This velocity of completed work helps the team self-assess how well the work process is functioning.

Agile development visuals boards are used to monitor work and give the team an instantaneous, visual measure of its progress. Due to the dependence on visuals, the Lean and agile methodologies have something in common; they both require unique spaces in the office.

Similar to Lean cell design, the team sits in close proximity to each other and close to the visual board. The team is moved out of its functional SILOs where it might overproduce (complete things before they are needed) and placed into the agile cell where they produce only what is needed for the current cycle. The space for agile development must be redesigned to put developers next to each other and next to the visuals that govern the work in process.

Fully implemented agile development is a highly scripted and disciplined practice. Much has been written about this method of development, and it carries its own vocabulary including scrums, scum masters, sprint ceremonies, etc. There is too much detail to repeat in this book. However, it is worth noting that the discipline in agile creates the standard work that helps the team achieve a level of discipline to achieve flow. The reliance on standard work is another similarity between agile and Lean.

THE POWER OF OBSERVATION AND LEARNING DONE UPFRONT

To initiate the flow, and to feed the flow found in development systems, there is a need to front load the process. Accuracy is required so the development team does not get bogged down with interruptions while waiting for work to be defined and loaded to the backlog. To avoid "starving the backlog" and providing enough work to keep the team productive, a new method is needed to accurately define the work in sufficient detail. Here we turn to a method borrowed from the design community.

Design thinking can be applied at the start of any agile process to define the work upfront. The method is used to truly understand what the user requires in the new design and to then translate the users' needs into tasks for the development team.

The practical technique within design thinking of making direct observations is practiced by IDEO, the well-known design company based in Palo Alto, California. The company designed a wide array of products including medical devices, toothbrushes, ski goggles, and the computer mouse. The company designers are so prolific that their output approaches nearly 100 new products every year. Many have seen the story of IDEO's deep dives in a 1999 television program done by Ted Koppel on the ABC television series Nightline. In the program, a weeklong deep dive is shown to gain insight into the IDEO design process. The specific design problem in the program is the shopping cart. All over the world, shopping carts are used by people on a weekly basis. However, shoppers live with the inconveniences of a product that does not work well for them. In their 5-day deep dive, IDEO designers utilize user observation and reveal many problems with existing shopping carts. The problems are exposed in order to think about what an improved cart would look like for the consumer in the store. One problem that many parents have experienced is safety. Reportedly, there were 22,000 child injuries every year due to tipping and other safety problems in existing carts.

The intent in design thinking is to use expert knowledge and to discern by direction observation, to discover the various problems with the design. The design team does this through interviews with people that are closest to the product. This requires going out into the field, finding those people, and talking to them. David Kelley, of IDEO, likens this as a social scientist, or anthropologist, who goes out into the field to observe the actual behavior of people. IDEO designers go into the field with cameras, notepads, tape recorders, or anything that works to capture the real problems that are occurring.

A key element at this stage is to define the true value of the product. What is the value that the storeowner requires? Shopping carts are a big investment for storeowners for something that has a limited life span due to damage and theft. Damage and theft represent wastes in the value equation that the designers need to minimize. The shopper has a different set of values: Safety of their children in the cart is important, as is the prevention of theft of purses or other valuables left in the cart.

The same attention to user-centered design is required of software development. Menlo Innovations uses a special role for the front end of the development process to ensure a user-centered focus called the High-Tech Anthropology® or HTA (High-Tech Anthropology is a registered trademark of Menlo Innovations, Inc). The HTA uncovers the true users' needs and translates them into story cards for the development team. The person in the role of the HTA writes tasks from the point of view of the user and translates them into user stories and tasks that can be completed by the team. This adaptation of the design thinking methodology defines for the developers the needs of the user.

The approach of using the HTA upfront in the development process ensures accurate requirements and places the users' needs front and center for the developers. As we will see in the case study, this places joy back in the software development process for both the users and the developers. The focus on value from the viewpoint of the customer, in this case the user, is a theme common to Lean and agile.

CASE STUDY – HOW RAPID CAN DEVELOPMENT BE?

In a converted space of an Ann Arbor, Michigan, parking garage basement there exists a very different software company. It is named after another innovative organization: Thomas Edison's labs in Menlo

Park, NJ, where the electric lightbulb and phonograph were invented along with thousands of other ideas.

This new innovative company is just 17 years old, but it has turned the software development world on its head with a new and different process. Menlo Innovations is a company that develops custom software for other companies and organizations. While a relatively young company, it has been recognized and awarded many, many times.

With less than 60 employees, it is a small company compared to many other Fortune 500 organizations. However, it has created a breakthrough approach to software development. This approach has transformed their company and radically changed its internal culture. In most software development organizations, there is a separation of duties and division of labor based on expertise that leads to towers of knowledge and experts in all aspects of database design, unique software languages, and development systems. Not at Menlo. Towers or knowledge are avoided, and expertise is readily shared. How is this accomplished? Work is done with two programmers working at one computer and one keyboard. A senior, more experienced programmer is often paired with a junior programmer. This allows knowledge transfer; pairs are also rotated weekly. By rotating pairs that often, knowledge and expertise is shared on a regular basis.

As a rule, software development is a date-driven and highly cutthroat industry. Individual developers are not valued because another developer with a specific skillset can easily be found to replace a tired and worn-out developer. There is plenty of competition from developers in other countries waiting to work at a fraction of the cost. Long hours of overtime and weekend blitzes to finish projects are commonplace. The value and integrity of the individuals who deliver the solution are often not respected.

At Menlo, all of this is different. Rich Sheridan, the CEO, had experienced the trials of software development for many years, and he suffered through long projects, plagued by delays and false starts but with the ever-looming deadline. He describes this process as a "death march" in which the developers work long hours under pressure to deliver a solution that may not meet the needs of the users. He wanted to do something different. He believed that development didn't have to be stressful, plagued by rework, and full of cost and schedule over-runs. So, he set out to change it. From this challenge, Menlo Innovations was born.

Rich Sheridan has talked and written extensively about the principles used to put joy in the workplace of software development. The methods of Menlo are transformational, and the company is noted more and more around the world. Menlo has hosted thousands of companies who have traveled from around the globe to the lower level of a parking structure in Ann Arbor to see Menlo work its magic.

Menlo has changed the way we think about space, visuals, the development process, and the culture of work. They have mastered agile software methods and applied many, many concepts that could be called "rapid development" in their workplace.

Every week the team members go through an entire development cycle, or what agile software developers would call a sprint or an iteration. That means that each week they plan, create unit tests, write code in "pairs," run thousands of tests, perform QA testing, and review the software with their clients. That is a one-week development cycle! They do this as a common practice every week of the year.

That is significant. Most companies go through very long development cycles that take weeks if not months to complete. They have not updated their methods and are using a development methodology called waterfall or phase-gate development. However, Menlo has a completely new approach. They are able to complete an entire development cycle every week. They do all of this in a 40-hour workweek, without anyone working any overtime.

The innovation has spilled over into many parts of their culture. To boost their efficiency and work time, they don't use email internally and have practically no internal meetings. There is no work done outside of work hours ever. Employees are also highly discouraged from checking in with the office while away on vacation.

How they manage to do all of this would take at least another book to describe. I would highly recommend getting a copy of Rich Sheridan's book *Joy, Inc.: How We Built a Workplace People Love* and reading the story from the Menlo chief storyteller himself.

SUMMARY

The One Main Thing – Agile and Lean are closely related disciplines and share many of the same concepts to limit the work in process and make development work flow.

STUDY QUESTIONS

1. How is the principle of focusing on the customer similar in Lean and agile?
2. How is focusing on one thing at a time relevant to Lean concepts?
3. What are the common elements in visual controls between Lean and agile?
4. How is continuous improvement accomplished in agile?
5. Why is empowering teams a central message in Lean?
6. How is the slow nature of waterfall development counteracted with Lean?
7. Why does moving learning up front streamline the development value stream?
8. How is design thinking leveraged in a development process to improve the customer experience?

NOTES

1 Authors note. A portion of Chapter 13 is taken from the article by Brower and Schipper, "The Baby & The Bathwater: Build on What You Know. Five ways Lean processes prepare teams for agile ways of working." © 2018 *360° Magazine*, Steelcase Inc.

2 Ibid.

APPENDIX A: TEMPLATES

A. Waste Tracking Template for Administrative/Office Wastes

Waste	Waste observed	Target condition (goal)	Improvement to be made
Defects			
Over-producing			
Waiting			
Non-utilized people			
Transport			
Inventory			
Motion			
Extra-processing			

SIPOC: *suppliers, inputs, process, outputs, customer*

Project name:		Process sponsor ⟶			Date
Value stream manager ⟶		Project manager ⟶			

Objectives:
clearly state what is to be accomplished ⟶
in the workshop include measures

Goals for process
improvement ⟶

Suppliers:	START WITH	Current state: Value stream map (high level) or list of process steps	END WITH	Customers:

Inputs:

Outputs:

Current metrics:

Information systems:

In scope:

Out of scope:

Issues and problems:

Workshop participants:	Decision panel participants:	Next steps:

Key dates		
Scoping		
Workshop		
Leader review day 30		
Leader review day 60		
Leader review day 90		

B. Scoping (SIPOC) Template

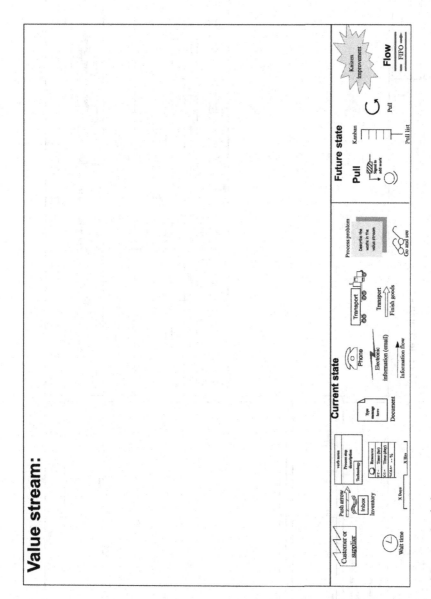

C. Value Stream Mapping Symbols

A3 project plan -
Kaizen

Overall project status

Indicate green or red status here --->

Business process
Process sponsor
Value stream manager
Project manager
Lean coach

Problem statement

Problem statement - what it is you want but don't have

Project objectives

List of objectives to be accomplished by this A3

Steering committee

Current state

Text, diagrams, value stream map, or picture

Future state

Insert picture, value stream, and or text here

Implementation plan

Task	Week of	11/03	18/03	11/5/03	1/22/03	2/5/03	1/26/03	2/26/03	3/4/03	3/11/03	3/18/03	3/25/03	Reason for red, comments	Responsible
1	Task													
2	Task													
3	Task													
4														
5														
6														
7														
8														
9														
10														
11														
12														
13														
14														
15														

Shaded area key: Green indicates task complete
Red indicated task late
Gray indicates original project plan
Finish task or milestone

Process measures:

Team members

Outcome Measures

Measure	Baseline	90 day target	30 day check	60 day check	90 day check	Reasons for not hitting your target measure and comments
1						
2						
3						
4						
5						

D. The A3 Project Plan

E. Workshop Checklist

Day 1

	Review training on Current state (30 min)
	Draw Current state – participants draw (4 hours)
	Identify waste using yellow stickies (1 hour)
	Discuss observations and put # on map (1 hour)

Output – Day 1

Training complete
Current state map
Observations
Observation # on map where it occurs

Day 2

	1st day debrief (.5 hours)	
	Future state training (1.5 hours)	
	Draw future state map – participants draw (4 hours)	
		Keep future state questions up while drawing
	Discuss future state objectives with owner (1.5 hours)	
		Decision panel prep – (.5 hours)
	Decision panel report out (1 hour)	
		Decision panel go/no go

Decision Panel prep

	1) Expected to engage with team re issues, questions, implications of map
	2) Expected to reach agreement w/team on map as is or as will be modified
	3) Be thinking about resource availability (best people)
	4) Define success for this process (what metrics most important to process)
	5) DP should ask team "what can you do in 30 – 60 – 90 days"

Think about what we can do if we just set a team on it (kill all else)

Output – Day 2

Training complete
Future state map
Objectives
Objective # on map where it occurs
Agreement (team & decision panel) for future state

Day 3

	2nd day debrief (.5 hour)
	Train on implementation planning tool (1 hour)

90-day rule
No (or minimal) IT rule

	Create implementation plan based on future state objectives (3 hours)

Priority of objectives

	Pre-decision dry run report out (1 hour)
	Decision panel report out (1 hour)
	Talk about next steps

When are update meetings

Who leads update meeting
Map on drive somewhere

Output – Day 3

A3s complete
Specifics of agreement with decision panel

Idea Boards

Idea Board

Focus area #1   Focus area #2   Focus area #3

Quick Wins   Ideas   Implementor   Due date   Status   Idea Activators

Team Projects   Parking lot

External Projects

Simple Kanban Boards

Basic Kanban Board

Backlog	Work in Progress	Review	Complete

Bibliography

Akers, Paul A. 2 Second Lean, How to Grow People and Build a Fun Lean Culture. Fast Cap Press, Ferndale, WA. Copyright 2014.

Bell, Steven C. and Orzen, Michael A. Lean IT, Enabling and Sustaining Your Lean Transformation. Productivity Press. Taylor & Francis Group, New York, NY. Copyright 2011.

Benson, Jim. Personal Kanban, Mapping Work. Navigating Life. Modus Cooperandi, Inc., Seattle, WA. Copyright 2001.

Brower, Tracy and Schipper, Timothy. "The Baby & the Bathwater. Build on What You Know. Five Ways Lean Processes Prepare Teams for Agile Ways of Working." 360° Magazine, Issue 74, Steelcase Inc. 2018.

Huthwaite, Bart. Lean Design Solutions. Institute for Lean Innovation, Mackinac Island, MI. 3rd Printing. Copyright 2004.

Huthwaite, Bart. The Rules of Innovation. Institute for Lean Innovation, Mackinac Island, MI. Copyright 2004.

Kelley, Tom. The Art of Innovation. Doubleday, New York, NY. Copyright 2001.

Kelley, Tom. The Ten Faces of Innovation. Doubleday a Division of Random House, Inc., New York, NY. Copyright 2005.

Locher, Drew. Lean Office and Service Simplified. The Definitive How-to Guide. Productivity Press. Taylor and Francis, LLC, New York, NY. Copyright 2011.

Mann, David. Creating a Lean Culture, Tools to Sustain Lean Conversions. 3rd Edition. Productivity Press. Taylor and Francis, New York, NY. Copyright 2015.

Morgan, James M. and Liker, Jeffery K. The Toyota Product Development System. Productivity Press, New York, NY. Copyright 2006.

Robinson, Alan G. and Schroeder, Dean M. The Idea Driven Organization. Berret-Koehler Publishers, Inc., San Francisco, CA. Copyright 2014.

Robinson, Alan G. and Schroeder, Dean M. Ideas Are Free. Berret-Koehler Publishers, Inc., San Francisco, CA. Copyright 2004.

Schipper, Timothy and Schmidt, Ryan. "Lean Methods for Creative Development. How to Rapidly Deliver Solutions and Capture Knowledge Using Lean Techniques." AME Target Magazine. Fourth Issue. Copyright 2006.

Schipper, Timothy and Swets, Mark. Innovative Lean Development. Taylor and Francis, LLC. New York, NY. Copyright 2010.

Schipper, Timothy and Swets, Mark. Single Point Lesson. Focused Learning on Vital Practices. "Lean Development." Target.ame.org. First Issue. 2010.

Sheridan, Rich. Joy Inc. How We Built a Workplace People Love. Penguin Group. New York, NY. Copyright 2013, 2015.

Shook, John. Managing to Learn, Using the A3 Management Process to Solve Problems, Gain Agreement, Mentor, and Lead. Lean Enterprise Institute, Inc., Cambridge, MA. Copyright 2008.

Ward, Al. Lean Product and Process Development. Lean Enterprise Institute, Inc., Cambridge, MA. Copyright 2007.

Womack, James P. and Jones, Daniel T. Lean Thinking. Banish Waste and Create Wealth in Your Corporation. Simon and Schuster, New York, NY. Copyright 1996.

Womack, James P., Jones, Daniel T. and Roos, Daniel. The Machine that Changed the World. The Story of Lean Production. Harper Collins Publishers, New York, NY. Copyright 1990 by Rawson Associates a Div. of Macmillan Publishing Co., reprinted edition by HarperPerennial in 1991.

Index

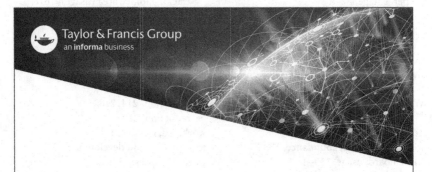

Printed in the United States
by Baker & Taylor Publisher Services